L.A. SHORTCUTS

The Guidebook For Drivers Who Hate To Wait

by
Brian Roberts
and
Richard Schwadel

Red Car Press
Los Angeles, California

L. A. Shortcuts
© Copyright 1989 by Brian Roberts and Richard Schwadel

First Edition 1989
10 9 8 7 6 5 4 3

Library of Congress Catalog Card Number
88-064173

ISBN 0-926055-00-3

Art Direction/Design by Hollowell Design
Illustrations by Jack Paul Miller
Edited by Dennis Graham
Photo by Ross Rappaport
Cover by Perry Van Schelt
Creative Consultant: Stella Wang

Printing 🏃 Graphics Management

Thomas Guide is reproduced with the permission of Thomas Brothers Maps.

For additional copies contact:
Red Car Press
Box 458
12228 Venice Blvd.
Los Angeles, California 90066

Table of Contents

Downtown Shortcuts

Hollywood Shortcuts

Valley Shortcuts

Westside/Beaches Shortcuts

It took the Viking II space probe nearly one year to complete the 142,000,000 mile voyage to Mars.

The inhabitants of Los Angeles drive that same amount every single day.

Introduction

THE BIG PICTURE

From the great chariots of Rome to the formula race cars of Indianapolis, history shows that there have always been just two kinds of drivers: The Leaders and The Pack. Each day over six million members of these two factions strap themselves behind their steering wheels and battle it out on the streets and freeways of Los Angeles. What results is a chrome-plated example of Darwin's Theory in action. Where you emerge on the evolutionary chain is entirely dependent on which group of drivers you choose to join.

WHICH KIND OF DRIVER ARE YOU?

Are you content to lounge in bumper-to-bumper traffic day-in and day-out, inhaling lethal doses of carbon monoxide? If so, then roll up your windows, turn on the air conditioner, and crank up the stereo. For you are one of The Pack. Should you choose to remain a member of this feeble fellowship, *L.A. Shortcuts* will have as much effect on you as yet another Freeway Condition sign on the Santa Monica Freeway. Invest your hard-earned dollars in extra cushy upholstery, for you have many long waits ahead and you're going to need it.

But if you look at driving as the ultimate sports challenge, punching through openings in traffic lanes like a halfback on his way to the Heisman Trophy, congratulations! You are a Leader, a true Shortcut Shark, and this book is for you. Shortcut Sharks instinctively know that to move is to live; to stop and lose momentum is to suffocate and die. To be this kind of road warrior is to adopt the principles of electricity — to always follow the path of least resistance — even if it takes you a few miles out of the way. A true Shortcut Shark would never sit motionless on any freeway when L.A.'s got more than 21,000 miles of surface street alternatives. After all, shaving precious minutes off your travel time gives you more time to stand in line at the bank!

RELIEF FOR THE ROAD WEARY

L.A. Shortcuts is the only driver's reference guide to defy the laws of physics by proving that the shortest distance between two points is <u>never</u> a straight line. Its routes have been painfully pried from obstinate Los Angeles natives. (In most cases, this rare breed would rather give up their first born.) It's the first road guide to commit these sacred urban shortcuts to print. Laboratory tested by the author's precision driving team of friends, professionals, and paid mercenaries, each route has been subjected to rigorous time and effectiveness tests. And we've found some good fast food along the way.

EIGHTY SUBURBS IN SEARCH OF A CITY

Let's face it, the Los Angeles area is so big that we had to draw the line somewhere. We chose the most clogged and congested areas familiar to the well-heeled urbanite. These areas are broken down by chapters: • Beverly Hills • The Canyons • Downtown • Hollywood • The Valley, and • The Westside and Beaches. At the head of each chapter is a handy reference map highlighting all of the shortcuts in that area with its corresponding page.

Each shortcut includes an illustrated map, best hours to drive each route, crucial tips, trouble spots to avoid, and various unsolicited editorial comments. Also included is the corresponding Thomas Guide map page (for quick cross-reference) as well as the approximate shortcut time. Most of the shortcuts in this book can be driven in either direction and picked up at any point along the route.

NO LICENSE REQUIRED

If you're able to drive and fumble with your stereo at the same time, you should be able to use this book. Keep it next to you while you're driving; it's the only shotgun companion that gives great directions and never talks back. So next time you're pondering why it takes you 45 minutes to get downtown when only yesterday it was a 20-minute breeze, remember this:

It's anarchy out there. The cardinal rule is: There are no rules.

But there are shortcuts.

The 11 Commandments
of the Road

The *California Driver's Handbook* does an adequate job of educating motorists in the art of driver's etiquette and traffic fundamentals. Though this is fine for members of The Pack, we Shortcut Sharks seek a much wiser sage for the knowledge demanded by our higher calling.

Do not be mistaken. The search for enlightenment is a lifelong endeavor. Nonetheless, we've taken it upon ourselves to provide this starter kit of rules and principles tailor-made for the novice Shortcut Shark.

1. IF IT'S WIDE ENOUGH, DRIVE IT!
Alleys, driveways, parking lots, gas stations. Be creative and do whatever it takes to get around a trouble spot.

2. EXPRESS YOUR FEELINGS.
Don't be afraid to show your displeasure at that Metalhead's blatant disregard for your road space! Define the limits of your intolerance according to the relative weight and size of your opponent.

3. DON'T MESS WITH THE PRO'S.
Tow truck drivers, messengers, and bus drivers all have one thing in common — they drive for a living in company-owned vehicles. You can use them to your advantage by trailing in their wake at a safe distance.

4. KEEP AN ALIBI HANDY.
Like an experienced pilot looking for a place to land in an emergency, always have a good reason for driving like a maniac. If nothing else, it will provide great entertainment for the arresting officer.

5. BUSY FEET ARE HAPPY FEET.
Pedals are designed to be pushed, pumped, and pounded. For those with automatic transmissions, we recommend the "two foot" technique.

6. EXERC-EYES!
Keep one eye firmly fixed on the road in front of you, leaving the other eye for utility purposes. This "roving eye" can alternate between gauges, your rear-view mirror, and unruly pedestrians.

7. YOUR CAR IS A SOVEREIGN COUNTRY.
Maintain a swift-handed dictatorship over all passengers at all times. Accept no uprisings. Passengers are merely baggage and have <u>no</u> <u>vote</u>.

8. WIELD, DON'T YIELD.
Your tax dollars pay for the road you drive on. You own it; take possession at all times.

9. FORGET FREEWAYS.
Back East they call them parkways. In the West they're known as freeways. We Shortcut Sharks call them "Plagueways." It's rumored that they're navigable during certain hours, although we're still trying to figure out when those hours are.

10. ALWAYS KEEP MOVING.
When the going gets tough, the tough make two lefts, a right, and a dash across a mini-mart parking lot. The object is to keep those tires moving in the general direction you're headed.

11. RESIDENTS TAKE PRECEDENCE!
Respect the locals when traveling through residential areas. You are an intruder who threatens their peaceful streets. Use extra caution when approaching blind driveways, and keep an eye peeled for kids. Irate homeowners have been known to lie in wait for speeding commuters and ambush them with rotten leftovers.

Getting to Know the Mean Streets

When it comes to driving in L.A., there's a lack of appropriate words to describe the people, places, and things that plague the Shortcut Shark. For this reason, we find it necessary to contrive a new vocabulary for these incessant road hazards. These terms won't be found in any respectable dictionary, but you will find them throughout this book.

Ambivalenties The species of driver who doesn't care where he's going or when he gets there; easily identified by the tendency to cut across four traffic lanes for no apparent reason.

Antsy Chow The habitually hungry maniac, whose relentless stomach pangs cause frequent U-turns near popular dining spots.

Brown Elephant The unsightly boil on the West Hollywood skyline, also known as the Beverly Center. The black hole of traffic snarls, it's a nightmare to drive near. We can only hope one day it will implode upon itself.

Commubots The stone-faced drones who unquestioningly travel the same road year in and year out. They are easily identified by their glazed expressions and strict adherence to all traffic laws.

Lefties Drivers who suffer from a penchant for making left turns at the most inconvenient locations, they are the most loathsome obstacles on the road. Lining up deep in turn pockets and ignoring "No Left Turn" signs is their favorite pastime. These people have never been instructed in the proper use of a turn signal.

Metalheads Known outside of their vehicles as blockheads, jarheads, lumpheads, and meatheads. Once behind the wheel, they <u>all</u> become Metalheads.

Metro Snail What can we say about the most ill-conceived, overpriced, and slowest-progressing project ever undertaken by the City of Los Angeles? Words elude us. Hence, our mollusk-like moniker for the much belated Metro Rail.

Olivehead The three-martini driver whose telltale weave from curb to curb requires nearby drivers to provide as much as twenty feet of crash space on all sides.

The Pack Them.

Plagueway An appropriate replacement for the now-archaic term "freeway."

Rabidasher The driver who appears to come from nowhere fast, lurching into your path at every corner, lane, driveway, or alley. They have no fear of violent death. If you're quick enough to spot one, get out of the way fast!

Reckless Traveling Disaster (RTD) It's hard to believe that these smoke-spewing, road-hogging, belligerent giants have anything to do with providing a public service. The RTD bus is a crafty opponent to be out-maneuvered at any cost. Dangerous, aggressive, and unpredictable, its record speaks for itself.

Republicruisers They're big, they're fat, they're ugly, and they're rude. But they're also rich and they drive huge cars. These are the people who don't just think they own the road — they <u>know</u> it! Unintimidated by mere mortals, *Republicruisers* will cut you off, double park, or run you over without as much as a second thought.

Righties These drivers have identical traits of the *Leftie* with one addition: They love to sit waiting for imaginary pedestrians at every crosswalk.

Shortcut Shark You.

Slomofo A strain of driver who perpetually motors a minimum of twenty miles an hour below the posted speed limit. A real bummer on a single lane road, these people should be banished to a life sentence on the Autopia ride at Disneyland.

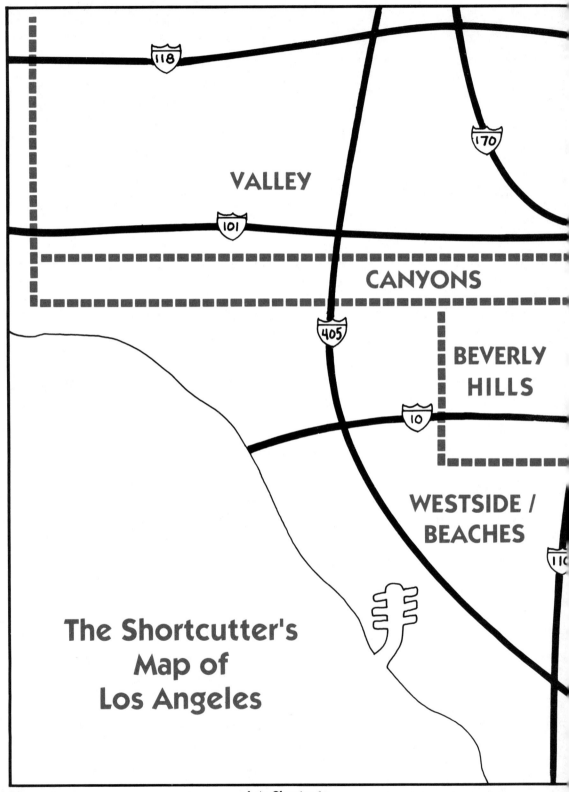

The Shortcutter's
Map of
Los Angeles

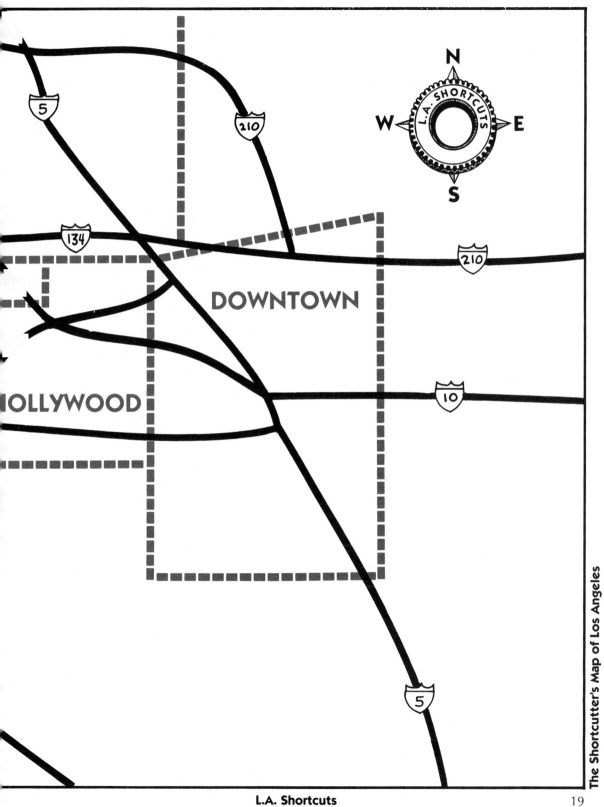

Beverly Hills

Exotic cars. Ultra-chic restaurants. Multi-million dollar mansions. These images flood the imagination at the mere mention of this city's name. Fortunately, Beverly Hills is one of L.A.'s tourist stops that lives up to its reputation. And why not? The money spent here annually on sports cars alone exceeds the Gross National Product of many Third World countries.

Though residents of Beverly Hills proudly cherish their city's image, the rest of L.A. regards it as a place where traffic moves at an escargot's pace. Wilshire and Santa Monica Boulevards share the burden of all the crosstown traffic. The remaining streets are laid out in a bewildering web of narrow, one-way avenues that seem better suited for sightseeing and shopping than efficient travel.

The parking sucks, too.

All this adds up to a challenge worthy of even the most loyal chauffeur unless, of course, he's memorized the following pages.

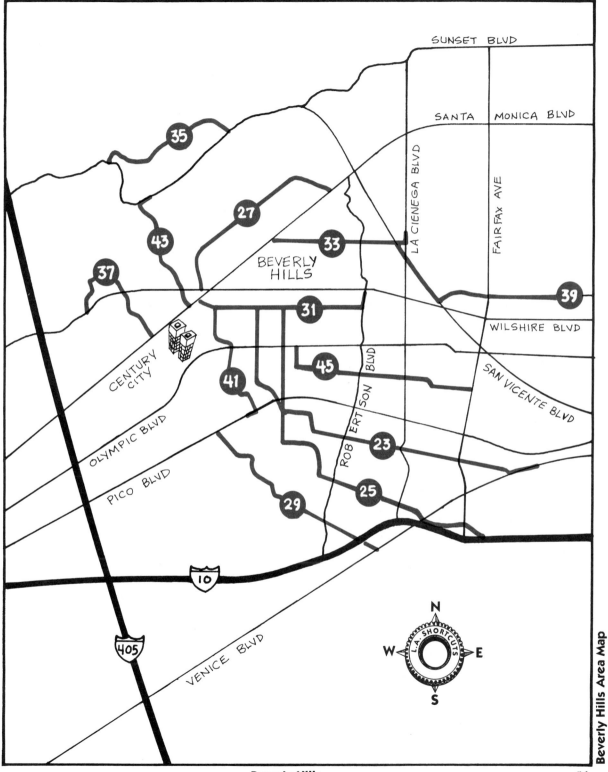

The Airdrome Express

(North/South Dogleg Approach to Beverly Hills)

SHORTCUT TIME:
6 minutes

T. GUIDE PAGE:
42

THE SCOOP
"Now boarding for Beverly Hills, Rancho Park, Century City and all points west —
last call for the Airdrome Express!" If Los Angeles had an efficient rail system today,
this call might be a favorite in any conductor's repertoire. But pipe dreams come
easily and rail systems don't. Though tracks were never laid down, Airdrome St. is
still one helluva ride between the Venice/Fairfax area and Rancho Park. Your accel-
erator pedal is the only ticket required while riding first class on the Airdrome Express. All aboard!

THE ROUTE
Westbound on Venice Blvd. veer west on Airdrome St. Go for about two uninter-
rupted miles to where Airdrome ends at Rexford Dr. Turn north on Rexford and go
one block to Cashio St. Turn west on Cashio and go about a half-mile until Cashio
ends at Roxbury Dr. Turn north on Roxbury and follow it into the heart of Beverly
Hills.

BEST HOURS/DIRECTION
This express line runs on time, all the time.

TIPS
Your locomotive could encounter a lengthy red light at Fairfax, but you'll steam full-
speed ahead after this. Watch your caboose between La Cienega and Robertson
Blvds., where the tracks narrow considerably. Be careful not to derail while crossing
over the many dips that pepper this run.

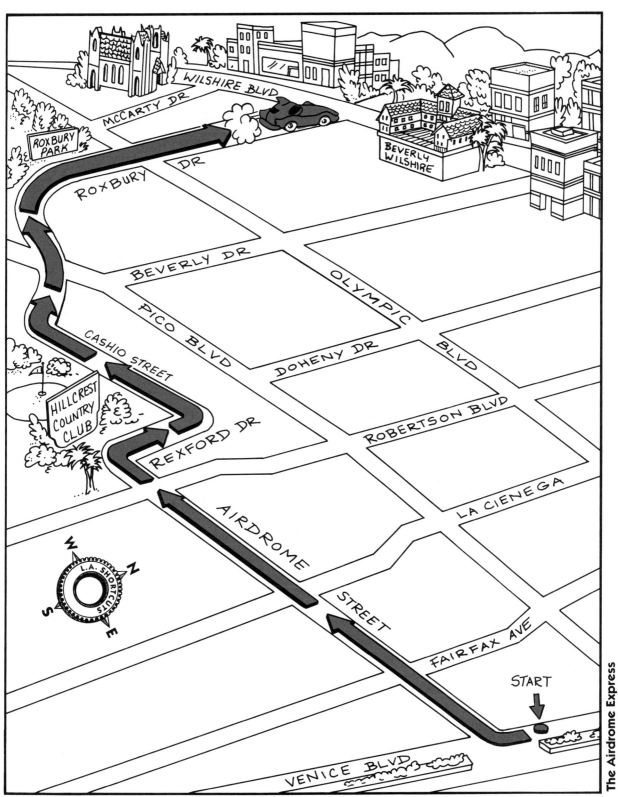

The Airdrome Express

Caddy to Caddy
(North/South Alternate into Beverly Hills)

SHORTCUT TIME:
4 minutes

T. GUIDE PAGE:
42

THE SCOOP

Throughout history, the greatest explorers and achievers have had a knack for cleverly summing up their exploits in just one memorable phrase. Armstrong had his "One small step." Hillary had his thought-provoking "Because it's there." And former President Nixon had his "I am not a crook."

Following in the tradition of these achievers, we, too, have a phrase that aptly characterizes our opinion of this route: "It's boring, but fast." Sure, you may not use it much now, but when you do, we're sure you'll praise our phrase.

THE ROUTE

Westbound on the Santa Monica Freeway get off at La Cienega Blvd. Although you won't see any street sign, you are now on Cadillac Ave. Follow Cadillac west as it turns into Hillsboro Ave. As Hillsboro bends to the left, it turns into Monte Mar Drive. Follow Monte Mar until you get to Beverwil Dr. where you can check your clubs at the Hillcrest Country Club, or continue north to Beverly Hills.

BEST HOURS/DIRECTION

Great any time, any day of the week.

TIPS

When getting off the freeway, make sure to avoid the right-hand lane because it's full of Metalheads turning north on La Cienega Blvd. After crossing La Cienega it's a smooth sail into Beverly Hills. The only difficulty you may encounter is staying awake.

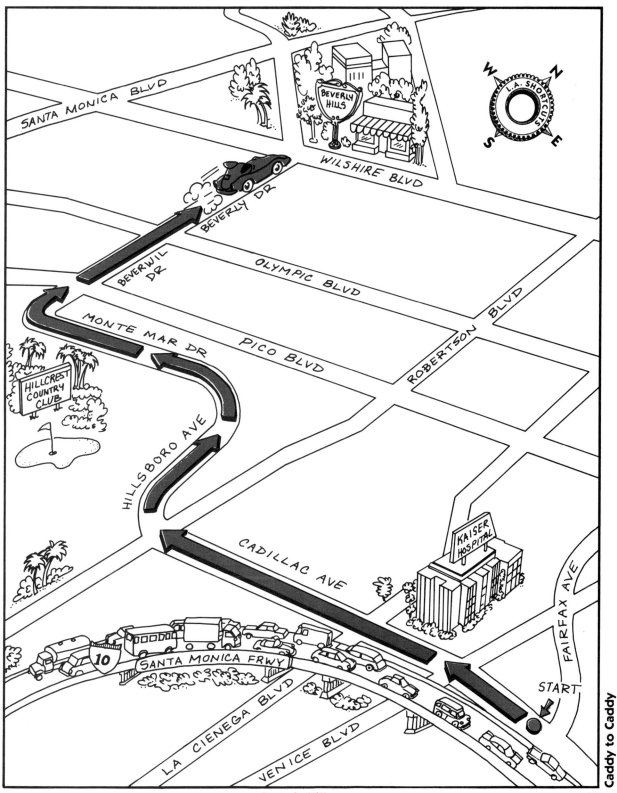

Caddy to Caddy

The Carmelita Stop-a-Go-Go
(Santa Monica Blvd. Alternate Through Beverly Hills)

SHORTCUT TIME:
6 minutes

T. GUIDE PAGES:
33, 42

THE SCOOP

Have you ever noticed that the joggers go faster than you do while driving Santa Monica Blvd. through Beverly Hills? It seems that when you cross the border into this little fiefdom everything is fashionable — except moving at a reasonable speed. But even if you haven't mastered the "California rolling stop," you'll appreciate our antidote for the daily Santa Monica Blvd. smogfest.

We don't call this the *Stop-a-Go-Go* for nothing. You'll work your way through 20 stop sign intersections, the fringes of a Robinson's parking lot and the entrance to the Beverly Hilton Hotel. But believe it or not, it's still faster than Santa Monica Blvd. at rush hour.

THE ROUTE

Westbound on Santa Monica Blvd., turn north on Palm Drive Dr. Turn west onto Carmelita Ave. and continue on Carmelita through 20 stop signs all the way to Wilshire Blvd. If you're headed toward Westwood, turn west on Wilshire. But if you want to get back to Santa Monica Blvd., turn south on Elevado Ave. and follow it through the Robinson's parking lot. Pass the entrance to the Beverly Wilshire Hotel. At Santa Monica Blvd., turn west and prepare to blend in with the crowd.

BEST HOURS/DIRECTION

This route is quicker only when the traffic is heavy on Santa Monica Blvd.

TIPS

Since Carmelita runs parallel to Santa Monica, you can pick it up any time the traffic gets unbearable. Be prepared, however, to find an ever-present Beverly Hills cop lurking in the shadows. We suggest keeping a convincing alibi handy. As you cross each intersection, look to your left and sneer with delight as you pass the turtles on Santa Monica Blvd.

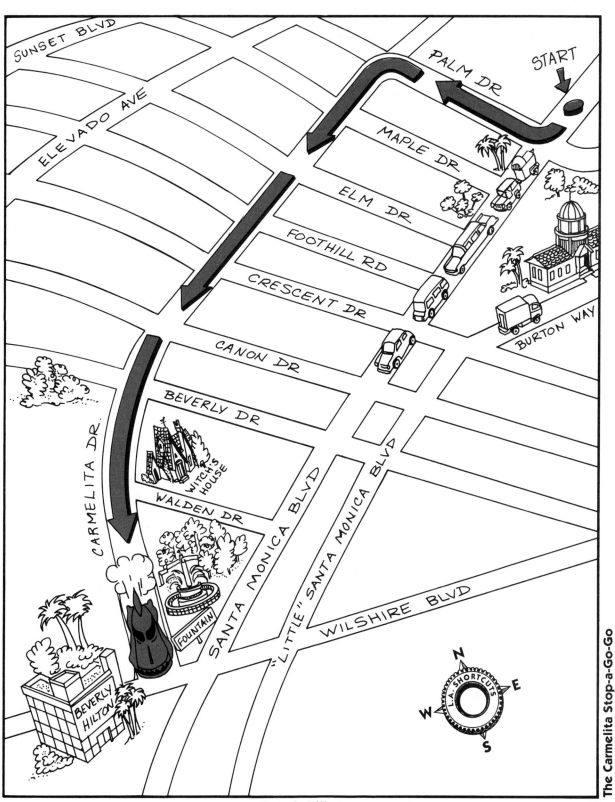

SUNSET BLVD

PALM DR

START

ELEVADO AVE

MAPLE DR.

ELM DR.

FOOTHILL RD

CRESCENT DR

BURTON WAY

CANON DR

CARMELITA DR.

BEVERLY DR

WITCH'S HOUSE

WALDEN DR

SANTA MONICA BLVD

"LITTLE" SANTA MONICA BLVD

FOUNTAIN

WILSHIRE BLVD

BEVERLY HILTON

N
E
L.A. SHORTCUTS
W
S

Beverly Hills

The Carmelita Stop-a-Go-Go

The Cattaraugus Cutoff

(Culver City to Century City)

THE SCOOP

Imagine that a cosmic fluke has occurred and you're the lucky recipient of a 9 a.m. starting time at Rancho Park, the world's busiest public golf course. But (expletive deleted).... the alarm went off late and you're buried deep in the sand trap at Venice and La Cienega! (Meanwhile three of your buddies are already headed to the first tee with drivers in hand.) You might try for a long shot with a hard poke up Motor, but we suggest you take a dogleg left with a short iron up *The Cattaraugus Cutoff.*

THE ROUTE

From either direction on Venice Blvd., go west on Cattaraugus Ave. until it ends at Beverwil Dr. Go north on Beverwil one block and turn west on Beverlywood St. Follow Beverlywood until it ends at McConnell Dr. Make a quick right and follow McConnell as it curves to the left and ends at Motor Ave. Turn north on Motor and cruise up to 20th Century Fox.

BEST HOURS/DIRECTION

This route cranks between Venice and Pico at all hours any day of the week.

TIPS

The intersection of Cattaraugus and Robertson tends to clog up with slow-going Lefties and Righties. Stay in the middle lane and blast your way across Robertson. You'll encounter about a half-dozen four-way stop signs, but keep moving and soon you'll be in beautiful Beverlywood. The streets get tight here, so hug the right curb. On McConnell you'll hit a "Y" where it joins Monte Mar. Veer to the left and you'll be at Motor in a snap. Watch for motorcycle cops hiding behind Winnebagos parked on Motor.

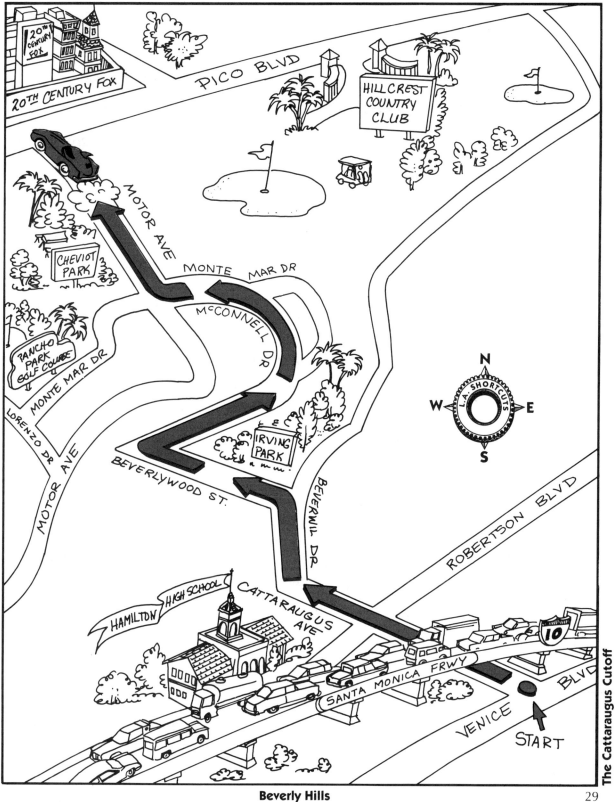

Beverly Hills

The Cattaraugus Cutoff

29

Charleville Stop-a-Go-Go

(East/West Wilshire Blvd. Alternate Through Beverly Hills)

SHORTCUT TIME:
6 minutes

T. GUIDE PAGE:
42

THE SCOOP

What the *Carmelita Stop-a-Go-Go* is to Santa Monica Blvd., the *Charleville Stop-a-Go-Go* is to Wilshire Blvd. It's a sister route that's a parallel paradise. When the traffic snarls on Wilshire, you can jack rabbit through Beverly Hills on a smorgasbord of stop signs and traffic lights. Of course, this route is invaluable for those who have mastered the "California rolling stop," but it's not exclusive to this elite group.

THE ROUTE

Starting at the intersection of Robertson and Wilshire Blvds., go south on Robertson one block to Charleville Blvd. and turn west. Stop and go on Charleville all the way through Beverly Hills until it ends at 'Little' Santa Monica Blvd.

BEST HOURS/DIRECTION

This route is usable during all hours, but really pays off during the rush hour crunch.

TIPS

For those with manual transmissions we caution against shifting past second gear as the stretches between stop signs are very short. Don't get caught behind any Slo-mofos, because there's no room to pass until you get to a major intersection. A few blocks before Doheny, try to time your stop-a-go-go schedule to make the green light. Above all, keep that utility eye peeled for the revered B.H.P.D., because, to the best of our knowledge, there are no donut stands in Beverly Hills.

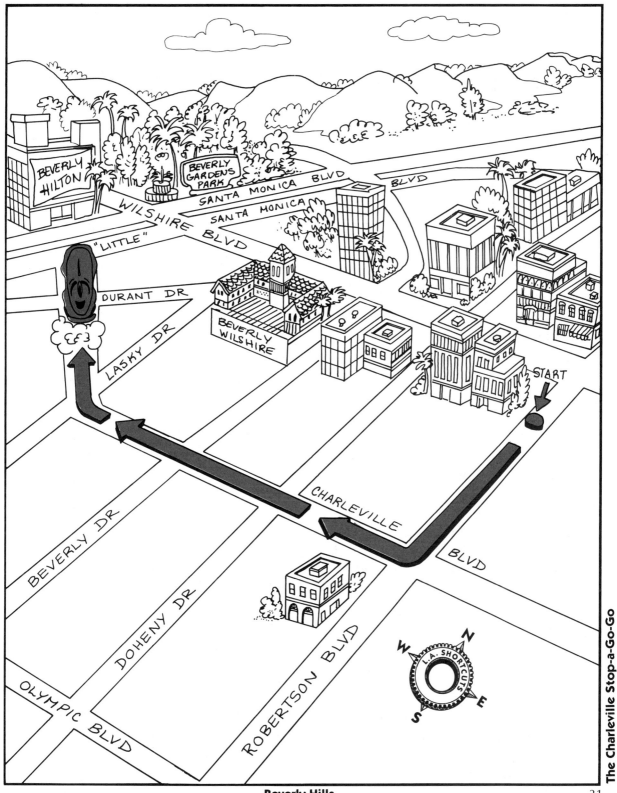

The Charleville Stop-a-Go-Go

God's Gift to Beverly Hills
(Mid-Beverly Hills East/West Corridor)

SHORTCUT TIME:
6 minutes

T. GUIDE PAGE:
33

THE SCOOP
When Lord Rexford of Beverlyshire convened an emergency meeting of the "Divine Order of Plunder Barons," it was in response to an unsavory uproar amongst the village lords. Apparently, there was no roadway fast enough for the peasants to trundle their cash into the itchy coffers of the Beverlyshire boutiques. In a burst of brilliance, Sir Burton of Whey (a Roads Scholar) suggested the construction of a pathway for the common man. He envisioned a spacious, no-nonsense byway piercing the heart of the township. His innovation survived. Today, when blowing through Beverly Hills, remember you're making great time only because Burton got his Way.

THE ROUTE
Southbound on La Cienega Blvd. turn west on Burton Way and continue on as it turns into 'Little' Santa Monica Blvd. in Beverly Hills. Continue through Beverly Hills and into Century City. You can even go as far as Beverly Glen before things get hairy.

BEST HOURS/DIRECTION
Burton Way smokes between La Cienega and Rexford at all hours. Traffic bogs down a bit in the mornings and evenings in either direction in downtown Beverly Hills and Century City, but it's still quicker than the alternatives.

TIPS
Northbound on La Cienega, you can't make a left turn onto Burton Way, so check your Thomas Guide and be creative. In downtown Beverly Hills you're going to have to play "thread the needle" to avoid the Righties and Lefties holding up traffic. Check out the Unocal station at the corner of Crescent Dr. and Burton Way. Resembling an experiment in concrete origami, this architectural acid trip is worth a drive in, fill up, and flash back.

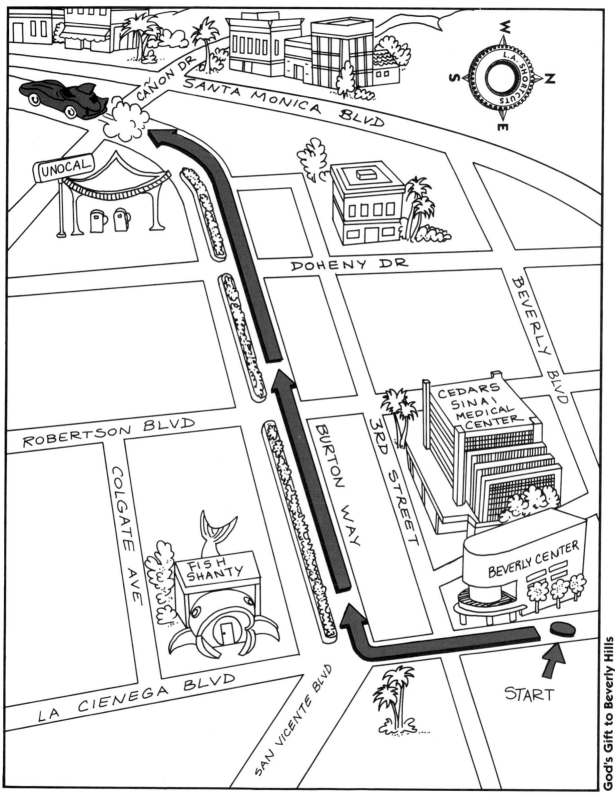

Beverly Hills

God's Gift to Beverly Hills

Lex Is More

(Beverly Hills Hotel/Benedict Canyon Bypass)

SHORTCUT TIME:
4 minutes

T. GUIDE PAGE:
33

THE SCOOP

Ever wonder why the residential streets of Beverly Hills are so wide? We do. Didn't city planners take the time to consider the plight of underprivileged motorists still driving on dirt roads? We don't think so. And how come after creating these revoltingly spacious boulevards, must drivers still endure the claustrophobic stampede of Sunset Blvd.? Well, we don't have to anymore. Just one long, oversized block north of Sunset lies the roomy remedy of Lexington Rd. It's a street where even us low-tax bracketeers can cash in on the asphalt bonanza of Beverly Hills.

THE ROUTE

Westbound on Sunset Blvd. turn north on Alpine Dr. and bear left at the fork in the road. You're now on Lexington Rd. Follow Lexington until it ends at Whittier Dr. From there, turn north and proceed one short block until the road forks. Bear left onto Monovale Dr. Follow Monovale and turn south on Carolwood Dr. You'll soon be at Sunset, way ahead of the Pack.

BEST HOURS/DIRECTION

You can take full advantage of this route during the twice-daily traffic snarls on Sunset between Benedict Canyon and Foothill. Though this shortcut works in both directions, we've found it more effective going westbound on Sunset.

TIPS

If you use this shortcut while going east on Sunset Blvd., beware of the difficult and time-consuming turn onto Carolwood Dr. It cuts across heavy oncoming traffic and should be performed swiftly and with an eye glued to your rear-view mirror. Once on Lexington, enjoy the tour of the area's mighty mansions. But don't look for any garbage cans. As Woody Allen once quipped, "There's no garbage in Beverly Hills because they put it all on television."

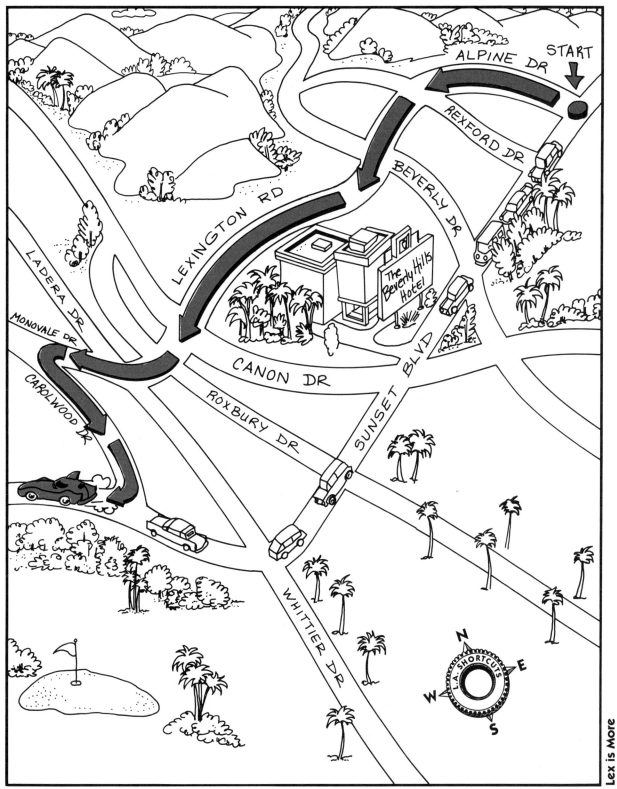

Beverly Hills

Lex is More

The Old Filmex Special
(Westwood to Century City)

SHORTCUT TIME:
6 minutes

T. GUIDE PAGES:
41, 42

THE SCOOP

Born in the leisure-suit days of the 1970s, the Los Angeles Film Exposition show-cased the cutting edge of cinematic art. Naturally, film buffs found the need to get from the posh eateries of Westwood to the even posher theaters of Century City. Regretfully, their dreams quickly faded to black as they ran smack into "Wilshire's Gate." A determined few found a happy ending in the rambling residential streets of Westwood, thereby pioneering the Filmex Special. Alas, the business suits of the 80's foreclosed on Filmex and replaced the cavernous cinema showplaces with shoe-plex theaters. Though the festival is finis, the route remains uncut.

THE ROUTE

Starting in Westwood, hop onto Lindbrook Dr. going east. Follow Lindbrook to just past Beverly Glen Blvd. where it ends at Devon Ave. Turn left on Devon and go two blocks to Strathmore Dr. Turn right on Strathmore and take it down the hill where it ends at Comstock Ave. Turn south on Comstock, and just past Wilshire, turn left onto Club View Dr. Follow Club View to its demise at Santa Monica Blvd. There, you're faced with the ugly task of getting into Century City.

BEST HOURS/DIRECTION

Getting out of Westwood on *The Old Filmex Special* is no sweat any time of day. At the intersection of Club View and Santa Monica, you'll hit a bottleneck that usually gets worse as you progress into Century City.

TIPS

Lindbrook has many stop signs, and it bisects busy residential streets. Be careful; the competition from other Shortcut Sharks is fierce. Take it slow on Club View's drain-age dips. Otherwise you'll be shaking hands with your transmission. After turning onto Santa Monica from Club View, jump into the right-hand lane to set yourself up for the critical turn into Century City.

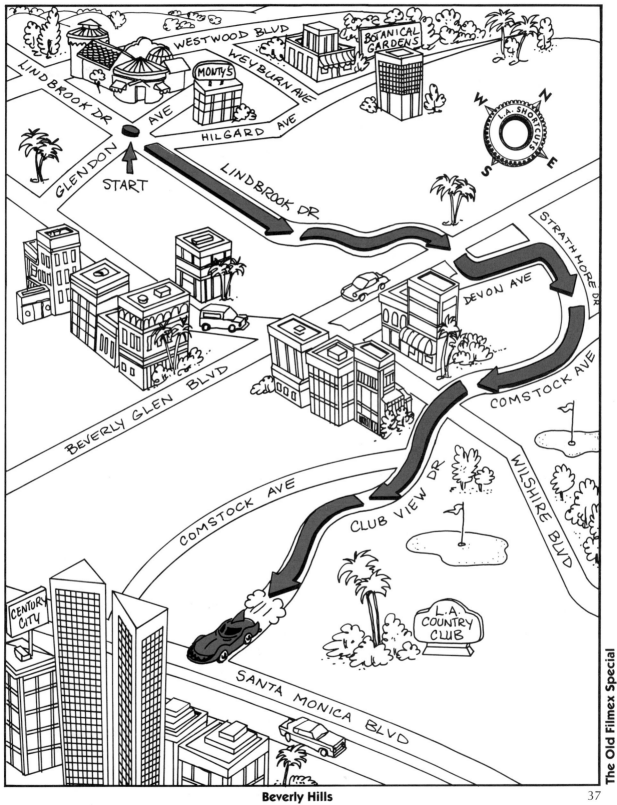

The Old Filmex Special

The Physicians' Pitch and Putt to Beverly Hills

(Hollywood to Beverly Hills)

SHORTCUT TIME:
11 minutes

T. GUIDE PAGES:
33, 42, 43

THE SCOOP

As you prepare to make a birdie putt on the 18th hole at the Wilshire Country Club, the silence is broken by the sound of your beeper. Skipping the lite beer at the clubhouse with your pals, you begin the agonizing journey back to your Beverly Hills office. Jerome the proctologist points out that it wouldn't hurt to take Beverly Blvd. Marty the podiatrist urges you to hoof it down 3rd St. But your attorney Bernie got an advance copy of this book, and he advises you to pitch and putt down 6th St. and Burton Way.

THE ROUTE

Starting at Rossmore Ave. and 6th St., go west on 6th all the way to San Vicente Blvd. Turn north on San Vicente and needle your way into the left-hand lane. Veer west onto Burton Way, which turns into 'Little' Santa Monica Blvd. Stop at the curb of your choice where your car will either be valet parked or ticketed.

BEST HOURS/DIRECTION

The optimal time to drive this route is during rush hours in either direction. But as an alternate to Wilshire, it's great any time.

TIPS

Remember to dodge the Lefties on 6th St., especially at Crescent Heights. Once on San Vicente, don't let any Rabidashers herd you onto the continuations of either San Vicente or La Cienega. If this happens, you'll get helplessly caught in the vortex of crazed shoppers being sucked into the bowels of the Beverly Brown Elephant (a.k.a. the Beverly Center).

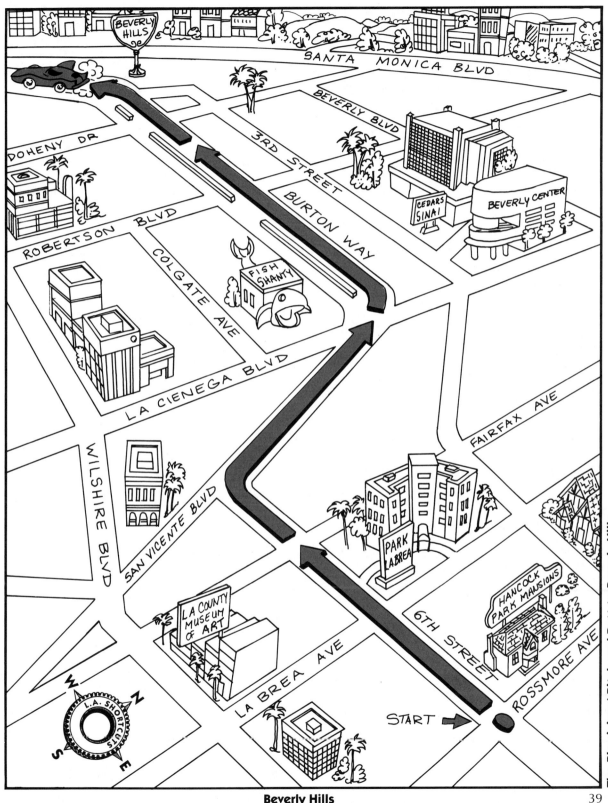

Pio Pico's Triple Bypass

(North/South Back Door Route Into Beverly Hills)

SHORTCUT TIME:
3 minutes

T. GUIDE PAGE:
42

THE SCOOP

In the rip-roaring 1870s, our beloved town was merely three pueblos in search of a Mission. Nonetheless, residents suffered the same traffic indignities that we do today. (If you think bumper-to-bumper exhaust fumes are bad, try riding hoof deep in road apples!) Even Pio Pico, the last Mexican Governor of California, was a victim of this malaise. When his instincts led him to the Hills of Beverly in search of some quick campaign funds, the local rumper-to-rumper horse traffic turned his gallop to a slow trudge. That's when he set off through the wilds to find a quicker way to town. His success was widely celebrated. And so the infamous "campaign trail" was born.

THE ROUTE

Eastbound on Pico Blvd. go one block past Century Park East and turn north on Beverly Green Dr. Turn left onto Hillgreen Place, then make a quick right onto Spalding Dr. At the fork in the road, bear right until the next fork in the road, where you'll bear left onto Moreno Dr. One block later, turn right on Lasky Dr. and follow until it ends at 'Little' Santa Monica Blvd. near Wilshire.

BEST HOURS/DIRECTION

Since this route travels through residential areas, rush hour traffic has little bearing on your travel time.

TIPS

If you're the first car at the intersection of Olympic and Spalding, be sure to rock 'n' roll back and forth to trip the signal sensors, or it'll be a long wait until the light turns green. You'll pass by the infamous Beverly Hills High where you can smirk or drool at budding tycoons honing inbred skills of looking keen and wealthy.

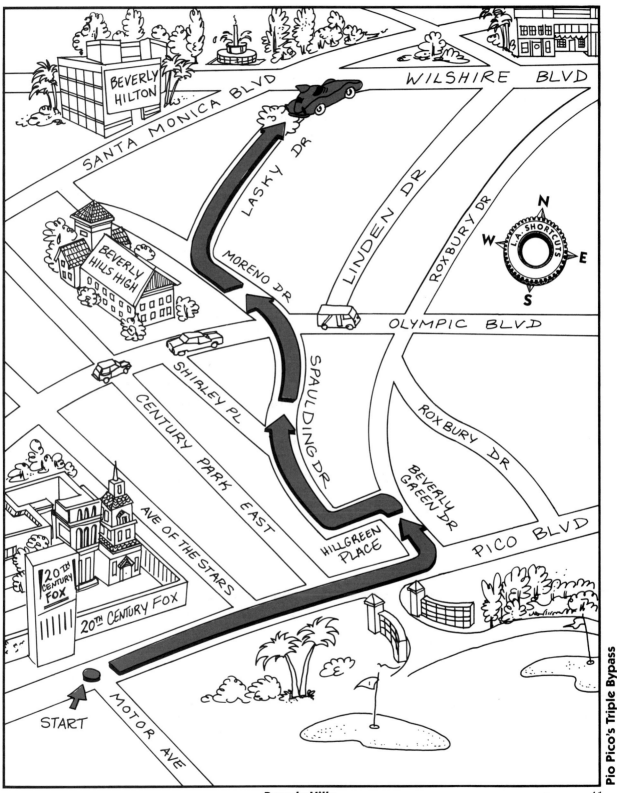

BEVERLY
HILTON

WILSHIRE   BLVD

SANTA MONICA BLVD

LASKY DR

LINDEN DR

ROXBURY DR

N

W   L.A. SHORTCUTS   E

S

BEVERLY
HILLS HIGH

MORENO DR

OLYMPIC   BLVD

SHIRLEY PL

SPAULDING DR

CENTURY PARK EAST

ROXBURY DR

AVE OF THE STARS

BEVERLY GREEN DR

20TH
CENTURY
FOX

HILLGREEN
PLACE

PICO BLVD

20TH CENTURY FOX

START

MOTOR AVE

Pio Pico's Triple Bypass

Beverly Hills   41

The Polo Lounger's Gallop to Century City

(Beverly Hills Hotel to Century City)

<u>**SHORTCUT TIME:**</u>
5 minutes

<u>**T. GUIDE PAGES:**</u>
33, 42

THE SCOOP
When the Hollywood trades announce that this week's megastar has "inked a multi-pic pact," chances are that the deal was consummated over tepid Eggs Benedict in the legendary Polo Lounge. This woefully overrated showbiz eaterie/dealerie has the distinct advantage of being situated a stone's throw from Century City. Quick to swoop down on big-buck opportunities, frantic entertainment attorneys beat a path between the two locations to "get it in writing" before their client can reach for the check. With such fierce competition, a slow trek through Beverly Hills could turn a hot deal into cold leftovers. So here's the gallop that legal eagles use to seal the deal.

THE ROUTE
Starting at the Beverly Hills Hotel go west on Sunset Blvd. to Whittier Dr. Turn south on Whittier and go four stop signs to the light at the corner of Whittier and Wilshire Blvd. Cut straight through the parking lot between Robinson's and the Beverly Hilton Hotel to Santa Monica Blvd. Then go west on Santa Monica Blvd. to Century Park East and pull into the personal parking space of your choice.

BEST HOURS/DIRECTION
This ruthless route can be affected by rush hour traffic in the shopping center area, but it's usually negotiable any time of day, except during the Christmas holidays.

TIPS
This is one of the few shortcuts severely affected by the holiday hordes. Since success depends upon the use of a department store parking lot, we recommend you sit out this shortcut until after the Christmas registers stop ringing.

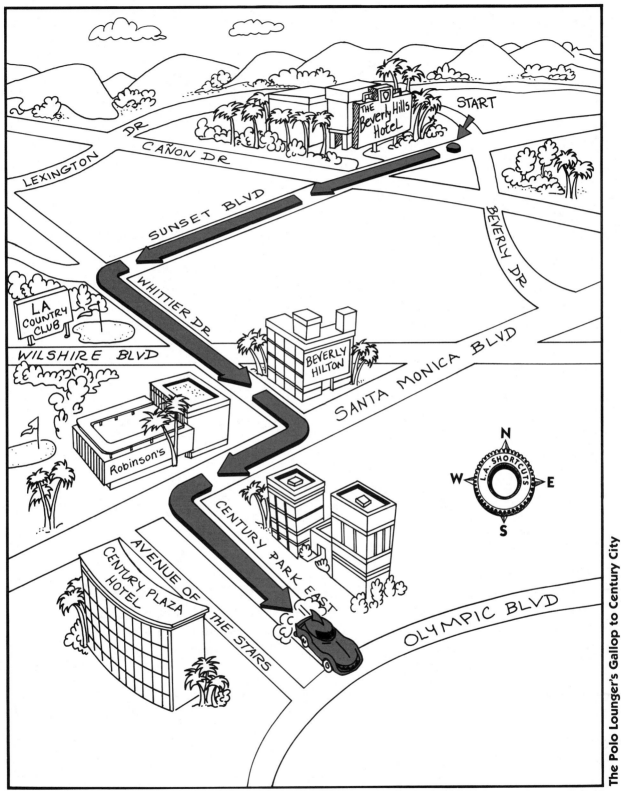

The Polo Lounger's Gallop to Century City

Whit's-Worth It

(East/West Wilshire Blvd. Alternate)

THE SCOOP

Shortcutter's log: Stardate 1990. Wedged between two intergalactic boulevards is an unspoiled, dilithium crystal gem. Its Earth coordinates lie on the Beverly Hills/L.A. border and its name is Whitworth Drive. This prized paragon will transport you from Beverly Hills to West Hollywood at warp speed. While the Klingon warriors crush each other on Olympic and Pico during rush hour, you'll beam right through the rubble with your shields down.

THE ROUTE

From the intersection of Olympic and Beverwil Dr., go south one block on Beverwil and turn east on Whitworth Dr. Only two stop signs block your trip to La Cienega Blvd. You can terminate there or cross at the stoplight and continue with ease to Fairfax Ave.

BEST HOURS/DIRECTION

You'll reach warp speed with this route during rush hours. Owing to its location between two major boulevards (Olympic and Pico), Whitworth is rarely populated with alien life forms.

TIPS

Don't let the lack of stop signs on Whitworth lull you into a false sense of security. The intersections that do have stop signs appear quickly. Unfortunately, two of those stop signs are planted at major intersections. Be prepared for a wait if you get stuck behind the Republicruisers at Robertson, La Cienega, or Fairfax.

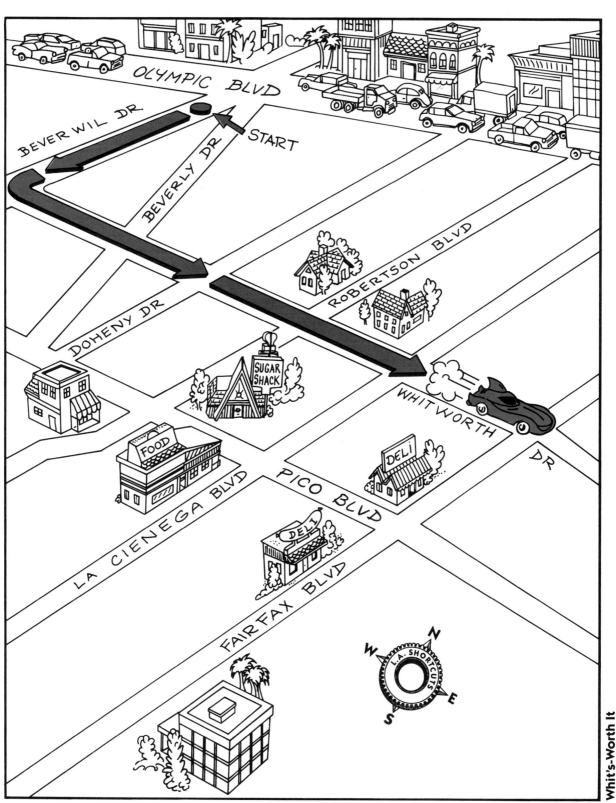

Whit's-Worth It

Canyon Routes

The mountains separating Los Angeles from the Valley are beautiful to behold, yet they represent a tragic flaw for commuters in the L.A. basin. Indeed, while the flatlands offer almost infinite commuting alternatives, there are less than a dozen ways to drive "over the hill." Getting from home to work and back results in a monstrous daily traffic crunch. Like clockwork, the two freeways and five major canyon passes overflow with those who believe there's no other way.

Though we can't dynamite another pass through the mountains, we can make the existing ones a little easier to traverse. Since the entry into the canyons is where the hordes convene, our shortcuts get you around these hot spots by taking you in the back way.

The few remaining unspoiled canyon passes we reveal in this section should be treated with the utmost reverence, for they are quickly heading in the direction of the dreaded list of endangered shortcuts.

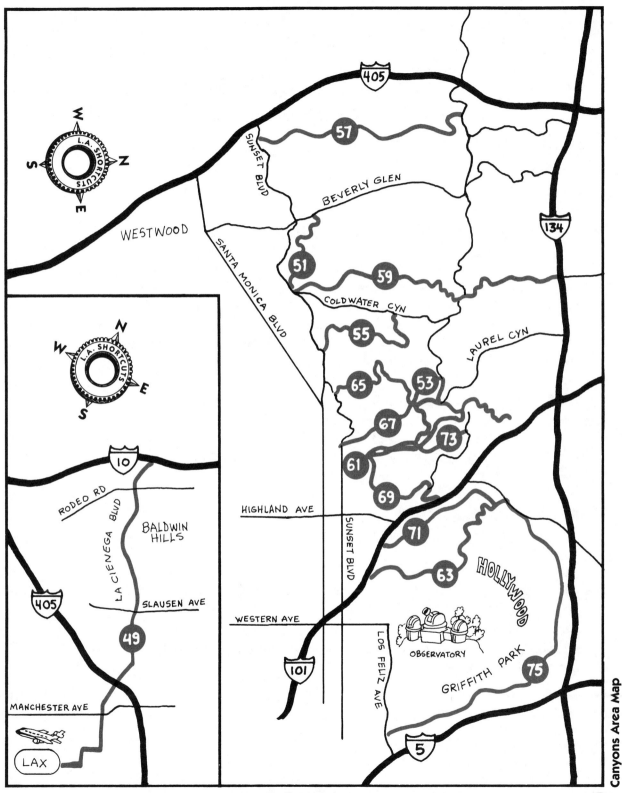

Canyons Area Map

The Airport Run
(Santa Monica/San Diego Freeway Alternate to LAX)

SHORTCUT TIME:
15 minutes

T. GUIDE PAGES:
42, 50, 56

THE SCOOP

Everyone hates it, but at sometime or another we all have to do it. It's the ghastly trip to the airport to pick up your long lost Uncle Waldo, who just happens to be passing through. The journey will no doubt include either the Santa Monica or San Diego Plagueways — each about as useful as the electronics system on a B-1 Bomber. Eventually, you'll have to get onto Century Blvd. — a street that Randy Newman may love to croon about, but is a nightmare to drive. Our *Airport Run* won't make the trip any less objectionable, but it will get you there faster. Unfortunately, you'll still have to suffer through a weekend with Uncle Waldo.

THE ROUTE

Southbound from the Santa Monica Freeway, get onto La Cienega Blvd. and fly south through Baldwin Hills. At La Tijera Blvd., turn west and crank down to Airport Blvd. Turn south at Airport and go about a half mile to 96th St. Turn west at 96th and grapple your way into the terminal of your choice.

BEST HOURS/DIRECTION

This run works great 24 hours, seven days a week.

TIPS

La Cienega between Washington Blvd. and Rodeo Rd. is full of slow moving shopper-gawkers in search of a bargain. Just south of Rodeo, hang on for a rootin' tootin' ride on the unspoiled La Cienega "Freeway." Once you're close enough to smell the jet fuel on 96th St., we recommend you park your car at Valet Air Park if you're going on an extended trip. They'll not only park your car but whisk you off to your airline in a New York minute.

Canyons

Beverly Hills Sheik Chute

(Southside Back Door into Beverly Glen)

SHORTCUT TIME:
3 minutes

T. GUIDE PAGES:
32, 33

THE SCOOP

Back in the late 70's, many a profit-rich oil sheik used this offbeat path to tool his Rolls between his Beverly Hills summer villa and Bel Air winter mansion. In the 80's, the OPEC cartel collapsed quicker than a Bedouin tent. Still, the sheiks used the route — between their Beverly Hills duplexes and their Sherman Oaks condos. While their Midas touch may have tarnished, they still strike it rich when they take the *Sheik Chute.* One doesn't have to be a desert fox to know that bypassing the rush hour snarl on Sunset Blvd. makes a wise investment.

THE ROUTE

Going west on Sunset Blvd., turn north at the Beverly Hills Hotel at Benedict Canyon. Go about a half mile to Angelo Dr. and then turn west. Follow Angelo until you get to a fork in the road at Brooklawn Dr. Veer left at the fork onto Brooklawn and follow it as you wind around the Westlake School for Girls. Right after the school you'll veer right onto Greendale Dr. and scoot one short block to Beverly Glen. Turn north on Beverly Glen and go over the hill to the Valley.

BEST HOURS/DIRECTION

This route only saves you time during heavy morning and evening rush hours. Still, it's a great deal in both directions.

TIPS

This shortcut can be a little tricky for first-timers, but there are road signs on Benedict Canyon that help point the way to Angelo Dr. From there it gets narrow and winding, but stick with it and you'll quickly empty onto Beverly Glen. There's some great greenery to see along the way, but the bigger distraction for the undisciplined comes when the road bends around the Westlake School for Girls.

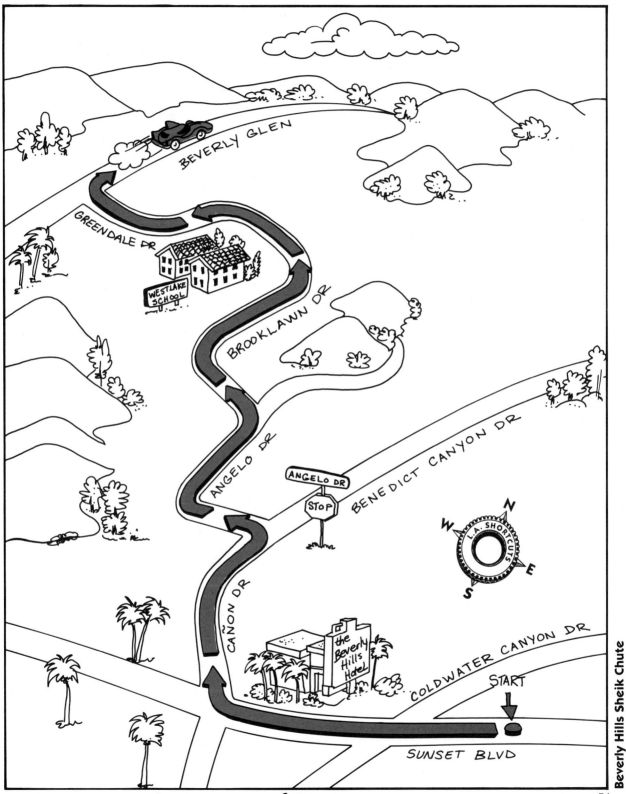

Book-Out on Lookout

(Mid-Laurel Canyon Bail-Out to Sunset Blvd.)

SHORTCUT TIME:
3 minutes

T. GUIDE PAGE:
33

THE SCOOP

How did Laurel Canyon get its name? Our guess is that it must have been named after Laurel and Hardy — because Laurel Canyon is such a joke. Sadly, the joke's on us. With 37,000 cars jamming down this narrow country road each day, we like to spell relief L-O-O-K-O-U-T. Detouring you around the loathsome section of the canyon south of Mulholland and into the back of the backwoods, this shortcut should prove both quaint and quick.

THE ROUTE

Northbound on Laurel Canyon Blvd. turn west when you get to Lookout Mountain Ave. Zip up the hill, and at the first fork, veer right onto Wonderland Ave. In one block there will be another fork where you should veer right onto Laurel Pass Ave. It's a straight shot up the hill to Mulholland Dr. where you can go east to Coldwater Canyon Dr. or west to rejoin Laurel Canyon Dr.

BEST HOURS/DIRECTION

This is strictly a rush hour route — good in either direction.

TIPS

During rush hour, it's a hassle getting to and from this shortcut, but be patient, because it's better than getting stuck in the canyon. Slow down on Wonderland Ave. at the schoolyard where you'll run into angst-ridden mothers in Volvos hell bent on snatching up their rug rats. Though Lookout and Wonderland are winding residential streets, you should still be able to kick ass up Laurel Pass.

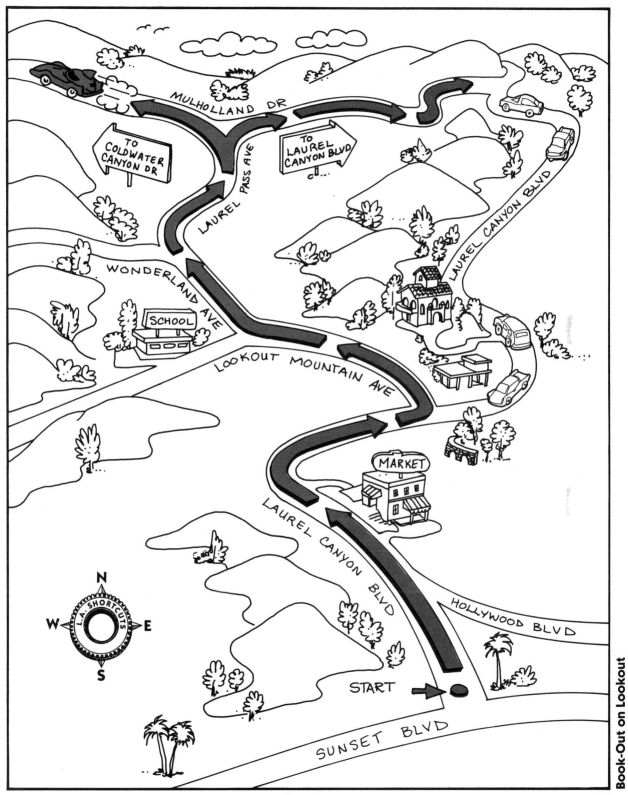

TO COLDWATER CANYON DR

TO LAUREL CANYON BLVD

MULHOLLAND DR

LAUREL PASS AVE

LAUREL CANYON BLVD

WONDERLAND AVE

SCHOOL

LOOKOUT MOUNTAIN AVE

MARKET

LAUREL CANYON BLVD

HOLLYWOOD BLVD

N
W E
S

L.A. SHORTCUTS

START

SUNSET BLVD

Book-Out on Lookout

From Hot Water to Coldwater
(Southside Sunset/Coldwater Canyon Bypass)

SHORTCUT TIME:
5 minutes

T. GUIDE PAGE:
33

THE SCOOP
This clutchbuster makes mincemeat out of the dreaded Coldwater Canyon commute, an ordeal that saps vitality from all who undertake it daily. It bypasses the lion's share of the congested canyon and a chunk of Sunset Blvd. to boot. This lifesaver should definitely become a permanent warhead in your shortcut arsenal.

THE ROUTE
From Sunset Blvd., westbound as you approach the Hamburger Hamlet, veer to the right at the signal onto Doheny Rd. Follow Doheny for a few blocks. At Greystone Park turn north onto Loma Vista Dr. Go straight up the hill for all your transmission is worth until Loma Vista curves around and ends at Cherokee Lane. Go west on Cherokee until you get to Coldwater Canyon Dr. Then turn north on Coldwater to get to the Valley.

BEST HOURS/DIRECTION
Because you must traverse the valley side of Coldwater Canyon to reach the start of this shortcut, weekday mornings and evenings can be slow going. The route is never really crowded, though, and it's always the fastest alternative in either direction.

TIPS
Manual transmission owners beware! The Loma Vista ascent can make your clutch hotter than a fistful of jalapenos. On those rare rainy days, proceed with extreme caution to avoid sliding into an expensive Trousdale landscape. Around Cherokee, small cars will find it easier to slip through the brief stretch where the road gets a little narrow.

W N E S
L.A. SHORTCUTS

CHEROKEE LANE

COLDWATER CANYON DR

TROUSDALE ESTATES

LOMA VISTA DR

GREYSTONE MANSION

HAMBURGER HAMLET

START

DOHENY RD

SUNSET BLVD

Canyons

How the Other Half Lives
(San Diego Freeway/Sepulveda Pass Alternate)

<u>**SHORTCUT TIME:**</u>
12 minutes

<u>**T. GUIDE PAGES:**</u>
22, 32

THE SCOOP

If you were a gambler pressed to bet on the best way to get from West L.A. to the Valley, you would probably place your money on a modern 10-lane stretch of concrete rather than a rambling, rustic country road, right? Wrong! No matter how you throw the dice, when dealing with the 405 through the Sepulveda Pass, you always crap out. Here's an inside tip on a sure thing that always pays off: Roscomare Road. Cutting through one of the more exclusive residential areas of Los Angeles, this winding mountain road poses a true challenge for the adventurous urban trail-blazer: whether or not to stop for a lottery ticket at the market on top of the hill.

THE ROUTE

Beginning at Sunset Blvd. go north on Glenroy Ave. Turn north on Cascada Way and turn east on Bellagio Rd. Turn right on Chalon Rd. and continue north to Roscomare Rd., where you'll turn north at the little park. Follow Roscomare all the way to the top to Mulholland Dr. Turn east on Mulholland and go one long block to Woodcliff Rd. Get ready for your ears to start popping! Go north on Woodcliff and follow gravity to Valley Vista Blvd., where, after making a left turn, you'll find yourself at Sepulveda, many lengths ahead of The Pack.

BEST HOURS/DIRECTION

The best time to drive this route is going south in the morning and north in the evening. However, the 405 Freeway can be jammed at any hour for no particular reason. So keep your ears glued to your favorite traffic report for possible evasive action.

TIPS

This route is not for the acrophobic! It's steep and narrow, with cars parked on either side of the road. Fumbling with your stereo or this book while trying to negotiate this pass can be quite treacherous. Commit this shortcut to memory! And since the route cuts through an upscale rural area, keep your eyes peeled for deer, coyote, and brat-pack beer busts.

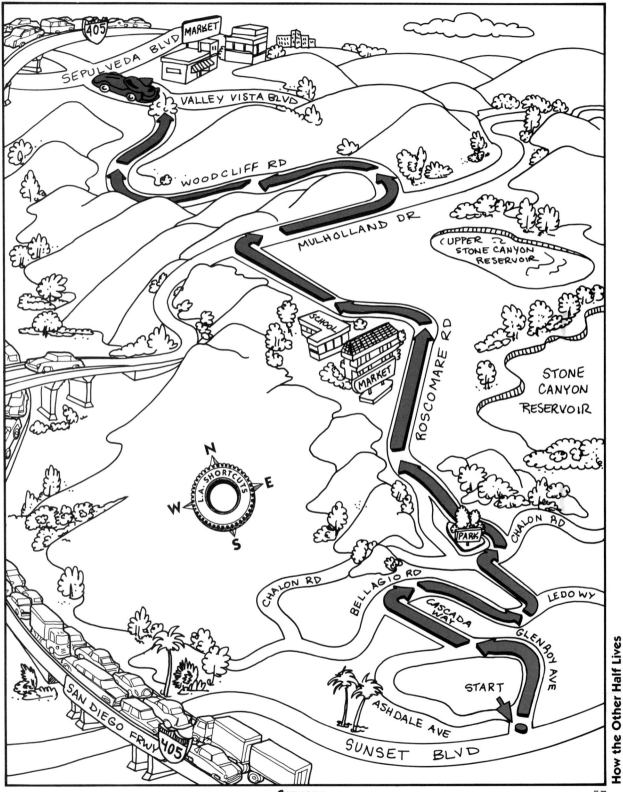

Kathy's Folly

(North/South Coldwater Canyon Bypass)

THE SCOOP

This shortcut is strictly for die-hard road warriors. A killer cross-country adventure passing through rugged terrain, *Kathy's Folly* leaves the southern half of the Coldwater Canyon commute in the dust. Venturing through the wilds of the Hollywood Hills on dirt and gravel roads, this route offers a rare glimpse of the way things were B.C. — Before Cars.

THE ROUTE

Southbound on Coldwater Canyon Dr., make a hard right on Franklin Canyon Dr. at the top of the hill. Take Franklin Canyon down to the reservoir to where it turns into a dirt road. Brave the dust and make your way around the reservoir until you meet the continuation of Franklin Canyon on the south side of the reservoir. Go past Lake Franklin Dr. and flow downhill to where Franklin Canyon joins Beverly Dr. Then continue south on Beverly to Sunset Blvd.

BEST HOURS/DIRECTION

Unless you're a four-wheel fanatic or Audubon Society member, use this shortcut during rush hour only. Warning: Do not attempt this route during or soon after a rainstorm. The dirt road turns into a muddy swamp that even the best four-wheelers can't escape.

TIPS

Franklin Canyon starts as a skinny passage and soon gets worse. Beware of reckless oncoming cars. Although we've never seen it closed, there is a gate blocking Franklin Canyon near the reservoir that may be locked at night. The rocky dirt road goes for about three miles and is a match for even the best suspension system. For those who choose to frequent this shortcut, we strongly suggest you invest in a flare gun for emergencies.

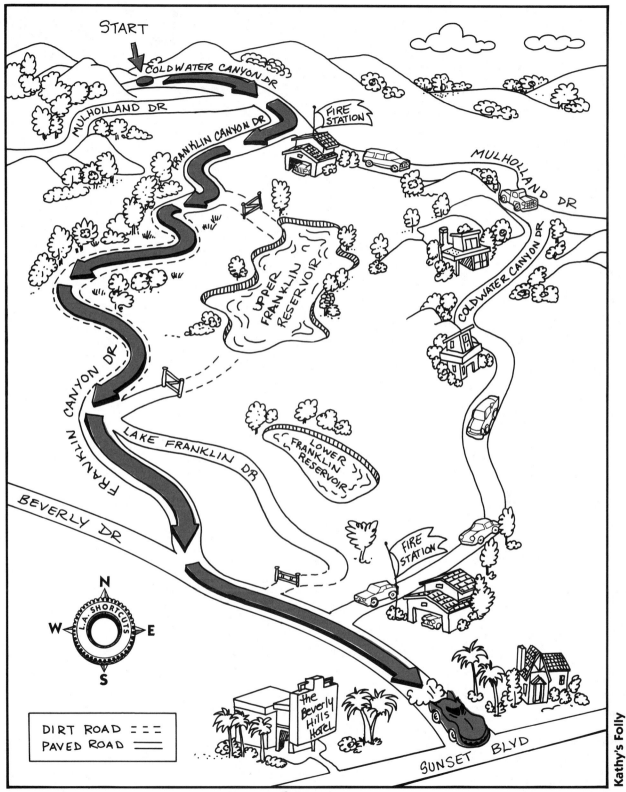

START

COLDWATER CANYON DR

MULHOLLAND DR

FRANKLIN CANYON DR

FIRE STATION

MULHOLLAND DR

COLDWATER CANYON DR

UPPER FRANKLIN RESERVOIR

FRANKLIN CANYON DR

LAKE FRANKLIN DR

LOWER FRANKLIN RESERVOIR

BEVERLY DR

FIRE STATION

N
W E
S

L.A. SHORTCUTS

DIRT ROAD = = =
PAVED ROAD ———

the Beverly Hills Hotel

SUNSET BLVD

Canyons

Kathy's Folly

Laurel Canyon Hideaway
(Southside Laurel Canyon Cutoff)

THE SCOOP
One of the hazards we faced in writing this book was enduring the unrelenting wrath of friends and family. They screamed that the publishing of shortcuts was nothing less than a threat to national security. Their warlike pursuit to dissuade us from our goal made us feel as if we were selling arms to the Ayatollah instead of scribing a harmless guide book. This climate of paranoia led some headstrong individuals to offer us bribes to keep their precious secrets safe from the public domain. The *Hideaway* is one of those secrets. Cutting off the dreaded Laurel Canyon clogfest, the *Hideaway* represents a triumph of private interests losing out to the public's need to know.

THE ROUTE
Westbound on Hollywood Blvd. go north on Nichols Canyon Rd. Go about one and a half miles up the canyon to Willow Glen Rd. and turn left. Follow Willow Canyon as it winds through the hills and flows into Laurel Canyon Blvd.

BEST HOURS/DIRECTION
This shortcut is good any time in either direction. Still, you'll get the biggest kick out of this Laurel Canyon escape hatch during peak rush hours.

TIPS
This route eliminates the most hideous parts of Laurel Canyon, but you can't avoid the traffic altogether. At the end of Willow Brook, you must rejoin The Pack and snake through the rest of the canyon like everyone else.

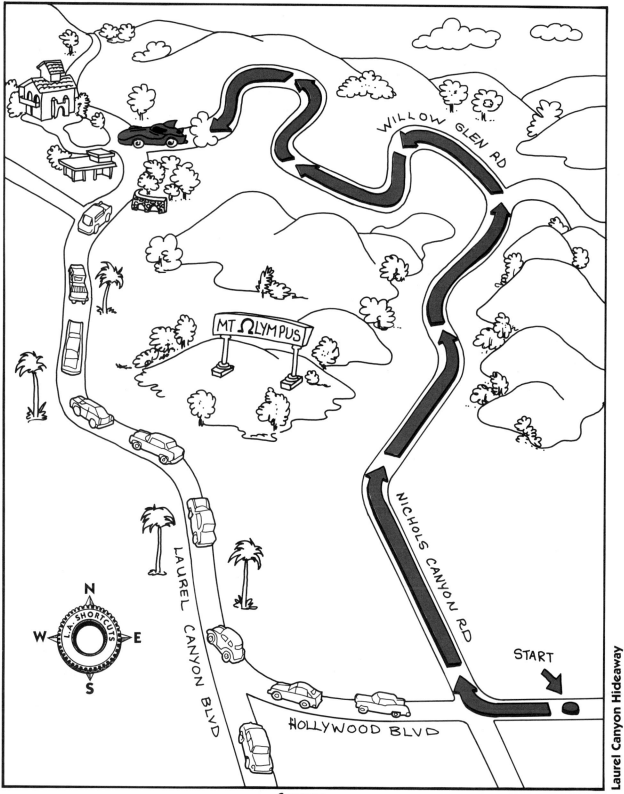

WILLOW GLEN RD

MT ΩLYMPUS

NICHOLS CANYON RD

LAUREL CANYON BLVD

N
W E
S

L.A. SHORTCUTS

START

HOLLYWOOD BLVD

Canyons

Laurel Canyon Hideaway

61

Out on a Ledgewood
(Cahuenga Pass/Hollywood Freeway Alternate to Burbank)

SHORTCUT TIME:
9 minutes

T. GUIDE PAGES:
24, 34

THE SCOOP
It's 4:49 on a Friday afternoon. You've skipped out of work early and can't wait to get home over the Cahuenga Pass and slap a couple of big T-bones on the grill. Suddenly, a traffic update informs you that 50,000 of your fellow citizens are parked on the Pass with the same idea. Though most Metalheads would prefer to slug it out, true Shortcut Sharks would rather switch than fight. This route shows off the relatively unknown Lake Hollywood area, and gets you home before your charcoal fizzles and the meat turns green.

THE ROUTE
Going north on Beachwood Dr. make a left at Ledgewood Dr. and follow it to Heather Dr. Make a left on Heather and then a hairpin right on Durand Dr. Follow Durand to Mulholland Highway. Take Mulholland west as it turns into Canyon Lake. Follow Canyon Lake past the little park and turn west on Tahoe Dr. Tahoe ends at Lake Hollywood Dr. Turn west there and follow Lake Hollywood around the reservoir. Follow the road up the hill and make a left at La Suvida. Follow La Suvida down to Primera and make a right. Then follow Primera a short distance to Lake Hollywood Dr. Just before Barham Blvd. make a right on the alley, and a left down to Barham Blvd.

BEST HOURS/DIRECTION
This shortcut is great during rush hour in either direction, but its calming beauty may seduce you into using it all the time.

TIPS
As you pass through the historic stone gates on Beachwood Dr., check out the Beachwood Cafe, where the wait is long but the chocolate shakes are great. The climb up Ledgewood will provide an award-winning view of the Hollywood sign, but don't let it distract you from the quick turn on Heather. The turn on Durand is hairpin-tight, but once you reach Mulholland you'll be treated to an inspiring view of Lake Hollywood. Once on Lake Hollywood Dr. keep a watchful eye out for joggers.

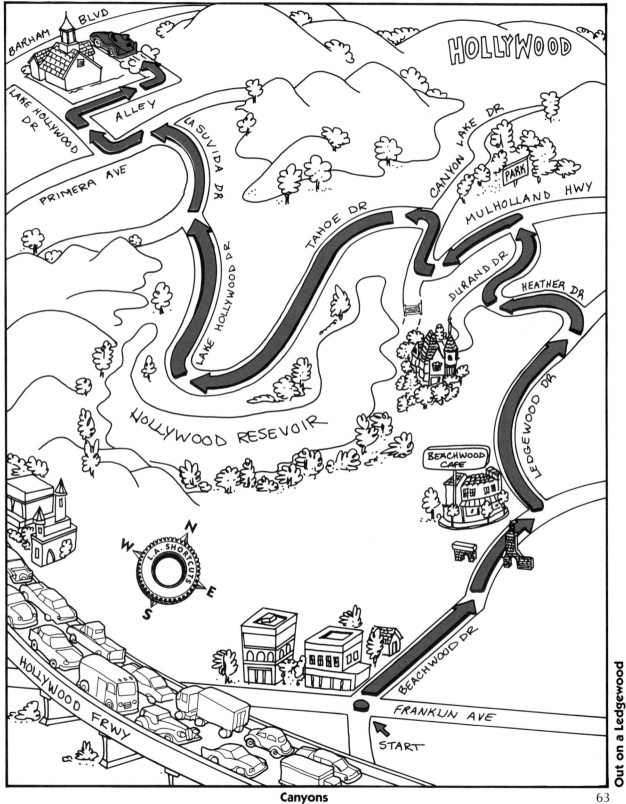

Out on a Ledgewood

Plaza Sweet
(Laurel Canyon/Sunset Blvd. Bypass)

SHORTCUT TIME:
10 minutes

T. GUIDE PAGE:
33

THE SCOOP
This three-alarm escape hatch will save you more in peace of mind than actual drive time. *Plaza Sweet* should be used in emergencies only. When your blood starts boiling at the thought of traversing Laurel Canyon and crawling down Sunset, a nice climb up Sunset Plaza won't seem so bad.

THE ROUTE
Southbound on Laurel Canyon Blvd., turn west onto Lookout Mountain Ave. Make an immediate left onto Stanley Hills Dr. Follow Stanley Hills as it winds around and intersects with Appian Way. Make a left on Appian Way (otherwise known as Sunset Plaza Dr.) and continue to wind your way down the hill to Sunset Blvd.

BEST HOURS/DIRECTION
Because this shortcut winds through the sleepiest residential section of the Hollywood Hills, it's good any time, but most effective in severe rush hours.

TIPS
This route is full of blind corners and dead-man curves so be careful! Flatlanders can gawk at city views and overpriced real estate they can someday aspire to — if they win the Lotto.

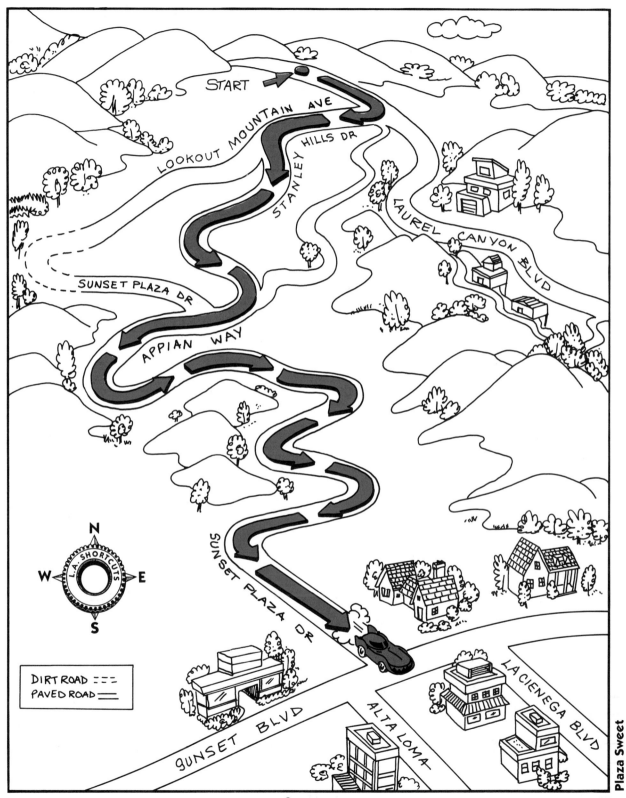

START

LOOKOUT MOUNTAIN AVE

STANLEY HILLS DR

LAUREL CANYON BLVD

SUNSET PLAZA DR

APPIAN WAY

N
W · L.A. SHORTCUTS · E
S

SUNSET PLAZA DR

SUNSET BLVD

ALTA LOMA

LA CIENEGA BLVD

DIRT ROAD ===
PAVED ROAD ——

Canyons

Plaza Sweet

The Poster Pass
(Hollywood to Universal City)

SHORTCUT TIME:
8 minutes

T. GUIDE PAGES:
33, 23

THE SCOOP

Plato was once overheard to remark, "All things are mere apparitions of their perfect form." Had he been contemplating the mountain passes that separate the San Fernando Valley from the rest of L.A., he would have been right on the money. Unfortunately, the great philosopher never was able to don his Ray Bans and crank his Porsche 911 through the canyons of Los Angeles... for there he would have found the perfect shortcut. Named for the director of photography who had to get from Laurel Canyon to the studios, this route helped provide the inspiration for writing this book. It is the authors' hope that it may now be passed from generation to generation.

THE ROUTE

Starting at Sunset Blvd. take Laurel Canyon Blvd. north to Mulholland Dr. Turn east on Mulholland and go one long block to Dona Pegita Dr. (Here we recommend Dramamine for those with weak stomachs.) Go north down the hill and turn east on Dona Lisa Dr. Follow Dona Lisa around the curve and turn east again on Dona Rosa. Make a westbound hairpin turn at Wrightwood Dr. and follow all the way down the hill. Turn east at Vineland Ave. to Lankershim Blvd. south and you'll soon be gazing at beautiful downtown Universal City.

BEST HOURS/DIRECTION

Use this route going north in the morning or south in the evening to best avoid the dreaded Laurel Canyon bottleneck.

TIPS

This shortcut takes a lot of practice and numerous clutch adjustments. But if you stick with it, wrong turns and all, it's possible to attain navigational nirvana. Take caution, though; this just isn't a good route for a van full of expensive electronics, kids, or anything else for that matter. On those five clear days a year, Wrightwood offers a wonderful vista of Burbank — as wonderful as a view of Burbank ever gets.

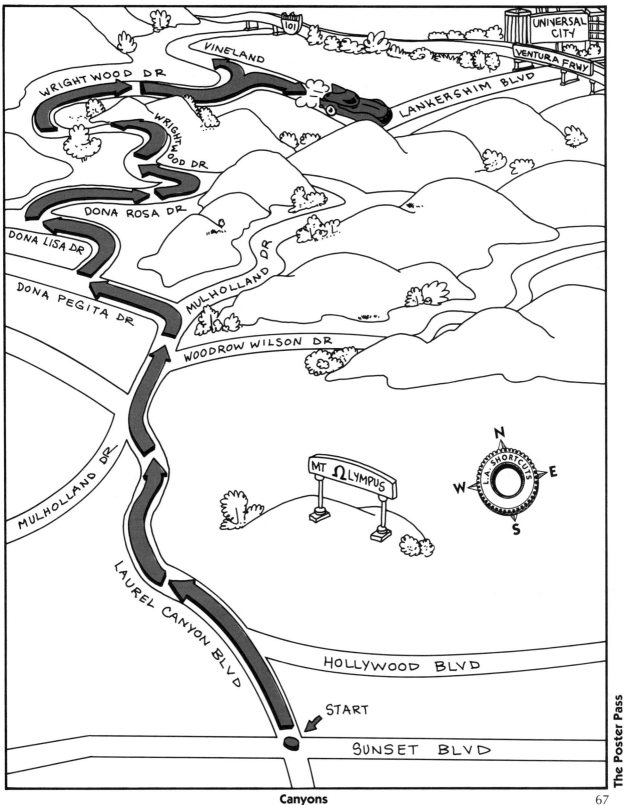

The Poster Pass

The Tinsel Town Trail

(Cahuenga Pass Alternate to Burbank)

SHORTCUT TIME:
6 minutes

T. GUIDE PAGES:
34, 24

THE SCOOP

Once upon a time you could board a quaint little red trolley for a serene ride through nature's link between Hollywood and the Valley, the Cahuenga Pass. Eventually they paved this paradise with a four-lane freeway, yet amazingly allowed the Red Car to continue along the median. It's all a memory now, leaving only a daily mesh of concrete and guard rails known as the Hollywood Freeway. It's a tough haul, and you've got to use any precious resource to your advantage. The Tinseltown Trail eliminates the southern leg of the Cahuenga Pass as well as the dreaded crossroads of Highland and Franklin — L.A.'s fifth most congested intersection.

THE ROUTE

Eastbound on Franklin Ave. turn north on El Cerrito Pl. Go one block and turn east on Hillside Ave. Go one block and turn north on the continuation of El Cerrito which turns into Outpost Dr. Follow Outpost and make the climb up to Mulholland Dr. Turn west on Mulholland Dr. and make your first right on Base Line Terrace. When Base Line ends, make a right onto Pacific View Dr. and follow around a big curve as it turns into Goodview Dr. On your way down the hill, Goodview intersects with Woodrow Wilson Dr. Turn east on Woodrow Wilson and follow even farther down the hill until you get to Cahuenga Blvd. West.

BEST HOURS/DIRECTION

The *Trail* is recommended only during rush hour, traveling either direction.

TIPS

Bring your oxygen tank for the straight blast up Outpost. This is not a good shortcut for those with feeble feet, lungs, or hearts!

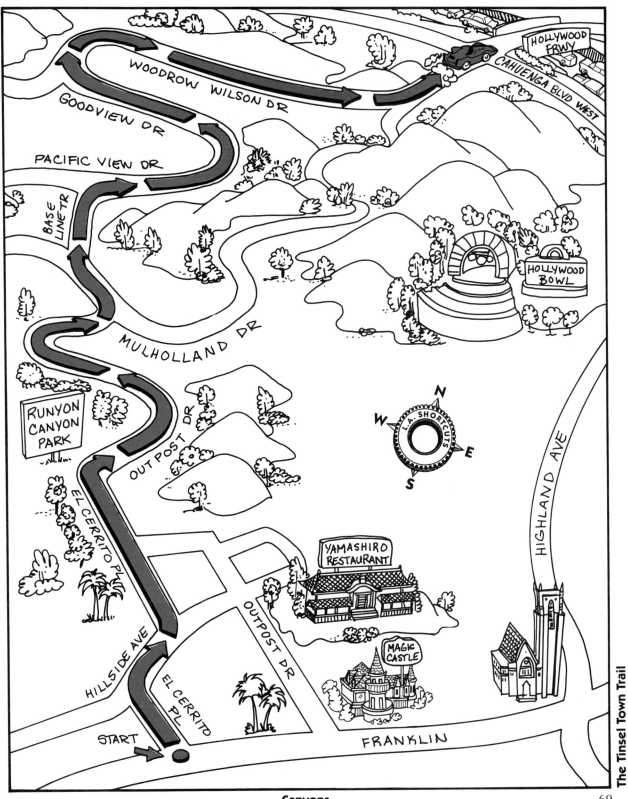

Canyons

The Tinsel Town Trail

Two to Toluca
(Cahuenga/Barham Intersection Bypass)

THE SCOOP

Toluca Lake: the eighth wonder of the world, for we wonder if there really is a lake behind all those Italian restaurants. It's a sure bet that if there is, Bob Hope owns it. The ninth wonder of the world is why anyone would want to work there, but they do. If you are a Tolucan toiler, getting there from the other side of the hill is a daily wrestling match. Luckily, our strategy will pin your opponent every time.

THE ROUTE

Follow Cahuenga Blvd. north in Hollywood as it curves around and parallels the Hollywood Freeway. When the crowd starts to back up at Barham Blvd., turn right at Hollycrest Dr. and bend around to the left. Follow Hollycrest to the intersection of Cahuenga and Barham Blvds. Turn east at Barham and go down the hill to picturesque Toluca Lake.

BEST HOURS/DIRECTION

Good news, bad news. This route really pays off during rush hour, but you can only use it going northbound towards Toluca.

TIPS

Due to the constraints of geography, you'll be stuck motoring on Cahuenga with The Pack most of the way. But once you hit Hollycrest, it'll be smooth sailing all the way. On Friday evenings you might want to indulge in a singles soiree for the recently separated at the infamous Oakwood Garden Apartment Complex.

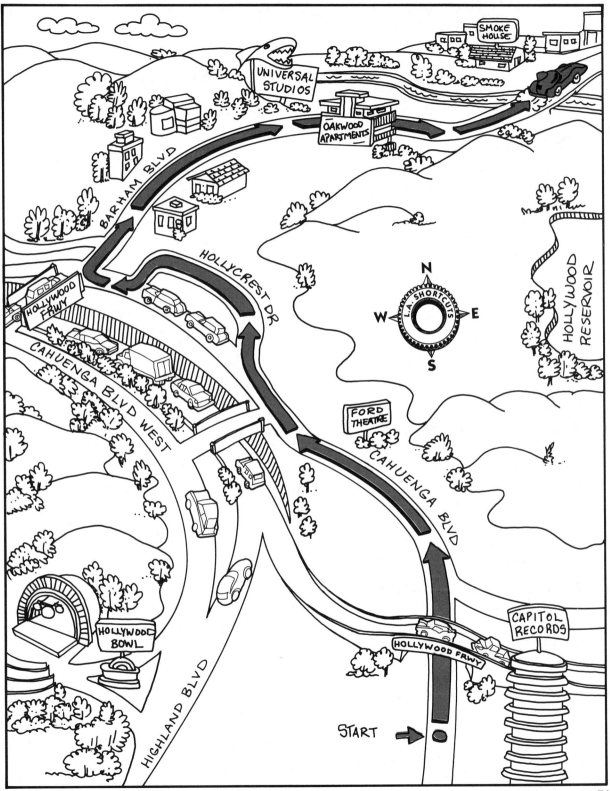

START ➡

Two to Toluca

Wood 'n' Nichols
(Southside Laurel Canyon Bypass)

SHORTCUT TIME:
7 minutes
(northbound),
5 minutes
(southbound)

T. GUIDE PAGES:
23, 33

THE SCOOP
Following in our tradition of staying off of Laurel Canyon at any cost, we offer you yet another alternate route: *Wood 'n' Nichols* through Nichols Canyon. Unfortunately the crucial leg of the route, Woodstock Rd., is closed to southbound traffic from 7 a.m. to 9 a.m. Monday through Friday. That's why this shortcut is divided into both northbound and southbound routes — proof positive that a great shortcut can sometimes become too effective for its own good.

THE ROUTE
Southbound: From Laurel Canyon Blvd. turn east on Mulholland Dr. and go one short block to Woodrow Wilson Dr. Turn east on Woodrow Wilson and wind around until you get to Nichols Canyon Rd. Turn south on Nichols Canyon and follow the hairpin turns down the hill to Hollywood Blvd.

Northbound: From Hollywood Blvd. turn north on Nichols Canyon and go straight to Willow Glen Rd. Turn west on Willow Glen and wind around until you come to Woodstock Rd. Turn north on Woodstock and go right up the hill to Woodrow Wilson Dr. Turn west on Woodrow Wilson one short block to Mulholland, then follow Mulholland until it intersects with Laurel Canyon Blvd.

BEST HOURS/DIRECTIONS
From 7 a.m. to 9 a.m. Monday through Friday, you must use Nichols Canyon. But at 9:01 a.m., start cranking southbound down Woodstock. There are no restrictions going northbound, so use the Willow Glen/Woodstock route any time in that direction.

TIPS
Nichols Canyon north of Jalima gets very narrow and twisting, so watch for road-hogging Republicruisers when heading into these turns. If you're going southbound, try to beat the light at Hollywood and Nichols Canyon. Otherwise, you could lose all the time you just worked so hard to save.

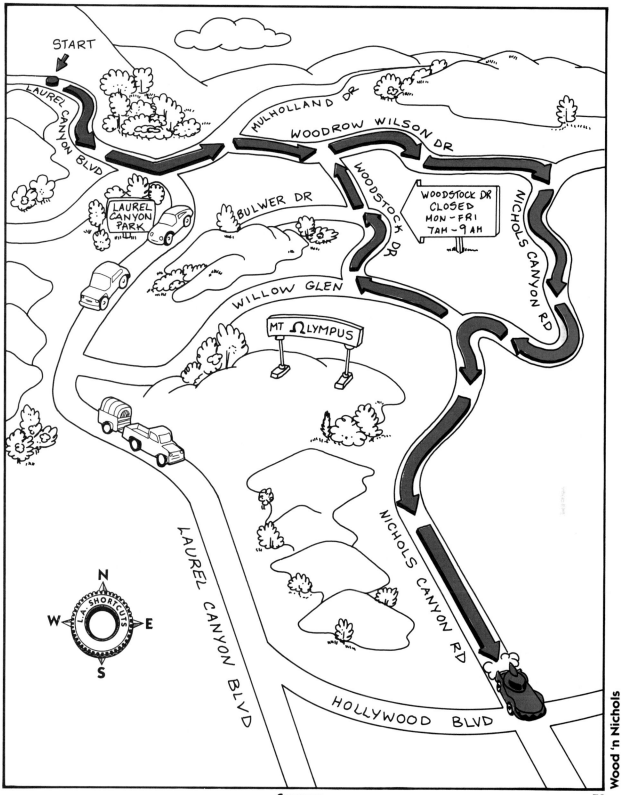

Zoo Zoo Zoodio

(Ventura/Golden State Freeway Alternate in Toluca Lake)

SHORTCUT TIME:
7 minutes

T. GUIDE PAGES:
24, 25, 35

THE SCOOP

What do golf, tennis, baseball, elephants, merry-go-rounds, miniature railroads, horse trails and cemeteries all have in common? Not much, unless you need to get from Burbank to Los Feliz and don't want to take the Ventura and Golden State Plagueways. You'll pass all of the above and the bumper-to-bumper rank-and-file as you breeze through the fringes of Griffith Park on *Zoo Zoo Zoodio*. This is the shortcut that Sunday drives were made for.

THE ROUTE

Going north or south on Barham Blvd. in Burbank, turn east on Forest Lawn Dr. As you pass Forest Lawn (the cemetery), it becomes Zoo Dr. Follow Zoo Dr. around the hill and past the Zoo. Although no signs say so, Zoo Dr. becomes Crystal Springs Dr., which winds past Harding Golf Course. At the merry-go-round, Crystal Springs becomes Griffith Park Dr., which goes past the miniature railroad to Los Feliz Blvd. Turn west on Los Feliz to get to Hollywood.

BEST HOURS/DIRECTION

This shortcut works better when going from Burbank to Los Feliz. It's still fast going the other way, but Griffith Park Drive takes a big detour around the zoo parking lot. Otherwise, this route is clear at all times on any day.

TIPS

Just as sure as there are sand traps on Griffith Park Golf Course, you'll stumble into an occasional speed trap on the many blind corners along the way. The posted speed limit is 20 m.p.h., so keep an eye open for friendly law-enforcement types. Other hazards to look out for are bikes, horses, and stray dens of cub scouts.

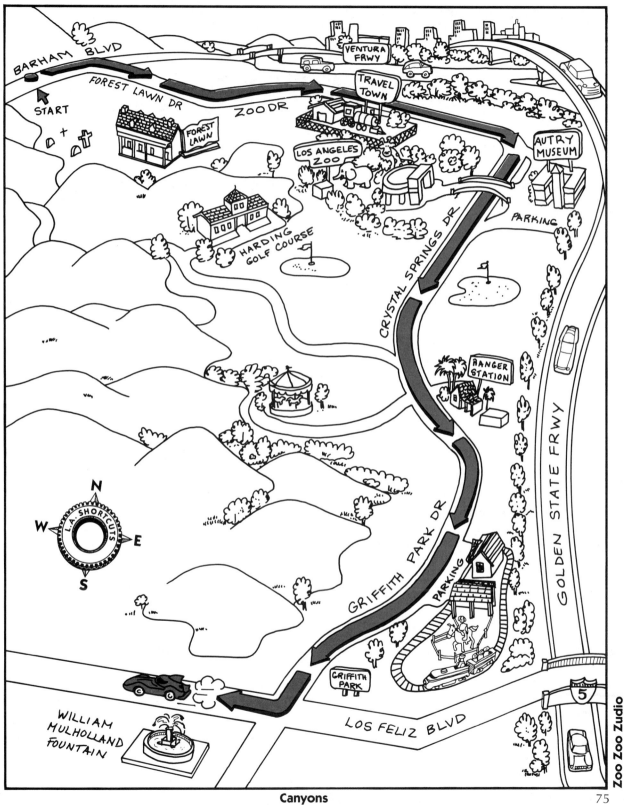

Canyons

Zoo Zoo Zudio

Downtown

Let's make this simple. Never enter Downtown any time before 10:30 in the morning, and make sure to leave by 2:30 in the afternoon.

Why? Driving in this area is a risky proposition at best. The streets are laid out in a twisted spaghetti-like maze, busses lurch out at you from all directions, pedestrians travel in unruly herds, and parking is a joke — with you as the punch line.

And that's on weekends.

Weekdays, take our advice and avoid the area altogether. Unless, of course, you receive a court summons, you absolutely can't resist a sudden craving for good Chinese food, or you somehow have drawn the misfortunate lot of actually having a job waiting there.

And so, with knuckles clenched to the steering wheels and dazed looks of endless gridlock to guide them, some 250,000 Commubots venture forth into Downtown every business day. If you are caught among this legion of brave and hardy souls, we offer our secret cache of Downtowners' shortcuts.

Think of these as sort of a little bonus you've earned.

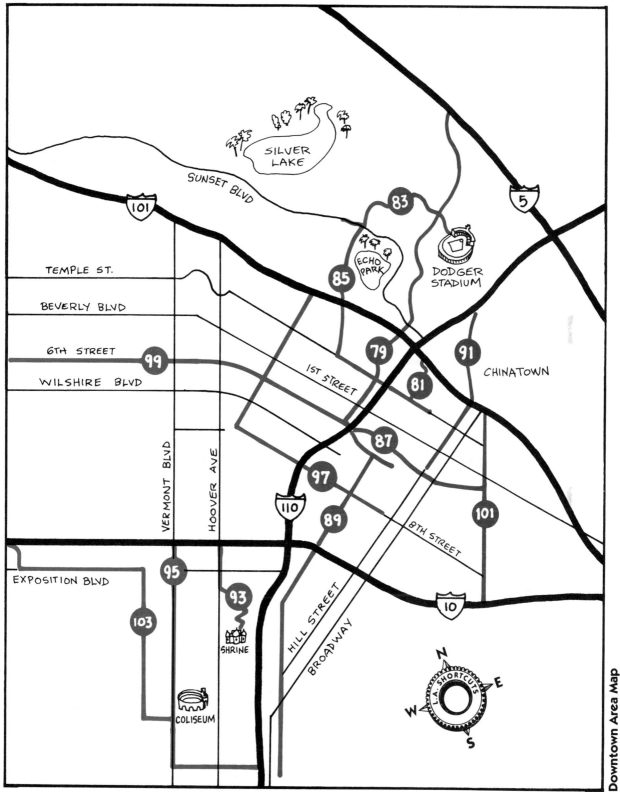

Downtown Area Map

Chris' Glendale Getaway

(Downtown to Glendale)

SHORTCUT TIME:
7 minutes

T. GUIDE PAGES:
35, 44

THE SCOOP
Deep in the bowels of a nondescript Downtown edifice lies the Caltrans Traffic Operations Center. Billed as a new frontier in traffic management techniques, the wall-sized freeway map of blinking lights and computer displays continuously updates officials on the latest conditions of L.A.'s beleaguered freeways. Every morning from 7:00 - 10:00 a.m. this high-tech marvel delivers the same bleak news: Traffic in and out of Downtown is at a dead stop. Big surprise. Any gypsy psychic with a second-hand crystal ball can tell you that. What neither the gypsy nor Caltrans can tell you is how to make the arduous commute from Glendale to Downtown in less than half an hour. Our friend Chris can, with her *Glendale Getaway.*

THE ROUTE
Take 5th St. west to Figueroa. Jump into the left-hand lane and follow the 6th St. West sign. Cross the Harbor Freeway and turn north on Beaudry Ave. Continue on Beaudry under the Hollywood Freeway and turn west on Sunset Blvd. Follow Sunset as it curves around to the right. Then turn right on Elysian Park Ave. Go one long block and then turn left on Stadium Way. Turn right on Academy Rd. and a quick left on the continuation of Stadium Way. Stay on Stadium Way until it runs into the Glendale Freeway.

BEST HOURS/DIRECTION
Great any time, any day except during Dodger games.

TIPS
Be sure to get into the left-hand lane when crossing Figueroa to pick up 6th St. West. Beaudry backs up a bit near 2nd St., but it smokes soon afterwards. Once you reach the tree-lined confines of Elysian Park it'll be open road the rest of the way. At Stadium Way you'll have an upper deck view of the Metalheads on the Golden State Plagueway. Make sure to jog left on Riverside Dr. at the bottom of the hill.

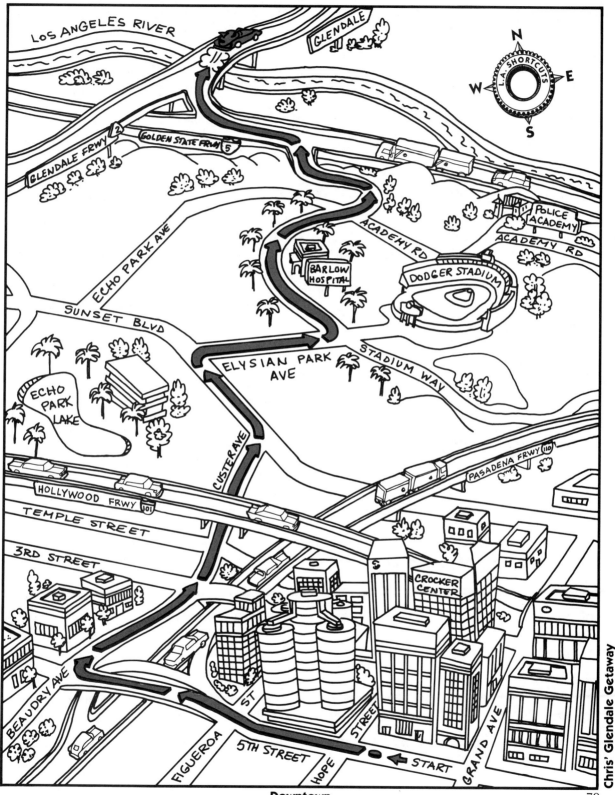

Chris' Glendale Getaway

Dewap Shoe-Bop
(Short-Range Northeast Figueroa Bypass)

SHORTCUT TIME:
1 minute

T. GUIDE PAGE:
44

THE SCOOP
One minute can get you a long way in this age of high-speed travel. If you're in a jet you'll travel eight miles. If you're in the Space Shuttle you'll log 450 miles. But if you're in a late model Chevy somewhere Downtown at rush hour, you're not going anywhere. That's why a short stretch can buy lots of concrete for your Downtown driving minute. As a workable alternate to Figueroa, Dewap St. may be short, but how sweet it is.

THE ROUTE
Northbound on Figueroa at 2nd St. bear right at the 1st St. exit sign (Dewap Rd.). Bulldoze your way across 1st St. and continue to Temple.

BEST HOURS/DIRECTION
This is a one-way route going northeast, but it's good all the time, especially when Figueroa is clogged.

TIPS
Finding Dewap Rd. for the first time will challenge the uninitiated, but once you find it, you'll *Shoe-Bop* till you drop.

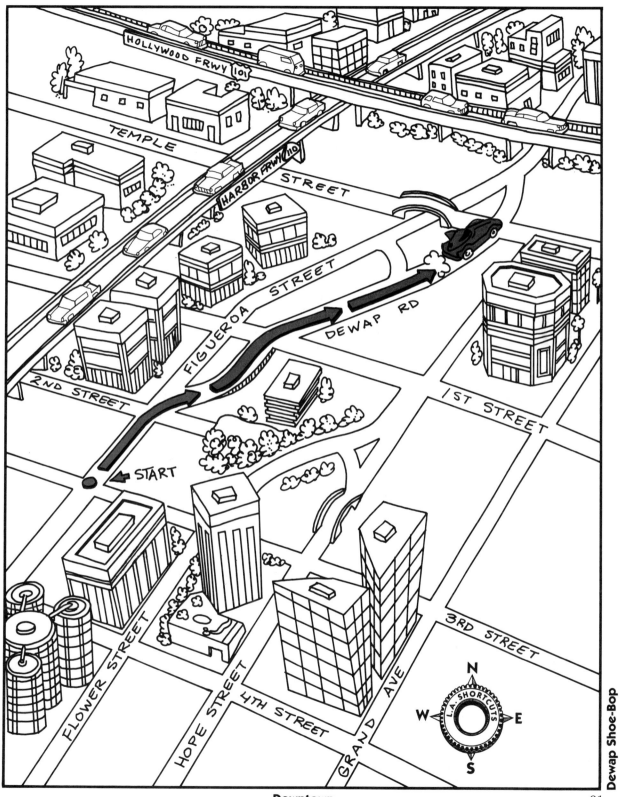

Dewap Shoe-Bop

Fernando, You Look Marvelous!

(Back Door Into Dodger Stadium)

SHORTCUT TIME:
9 minutes

T. GUIDE PAGES:
35, 44

THE SCOOP

To some, there's nothing finer than being perched on the third base line at Dodger Stadium with a spicy dog in one hand and a cool brew in the other. Unfortunately, getting to your $25 box seats in time to hear Mary Hart warble our National Anthem is harder than hitting a split-finger fastball. Let's face it, unless the Dodgers are in last place, there's always going to be traffic on game day. Our navigational formula is quite simple: crowd size = standings x team batting average.

THE ROUTE

Southbound on the Hollywood Freeway, get off at Glendale Blvd. Go north one block and make a quick right on Bellevue Ave. Turn left on Echo Park Ave. and follow Echo Park past the swamp called Echo Lake to just past Scott Ave. Veer to the right as it turns into Morton Ave. and follow Morton as it turns into Academy Rd. From there it's a line drive into the left field of Chavez Ravine.

BEST HOURS/DIRECTION

This shortcut is definitely a seasonal pass. But as the baseball season drags on longer each year, one day this route might yield a high average year round.

TIPS

Going north on the Hollywood Freeway, get off at Echo Park (bypassing Glendale Blvd.). Near Stadium Way, Echo Park widens — try to stay on the right to avoid the Lefties.

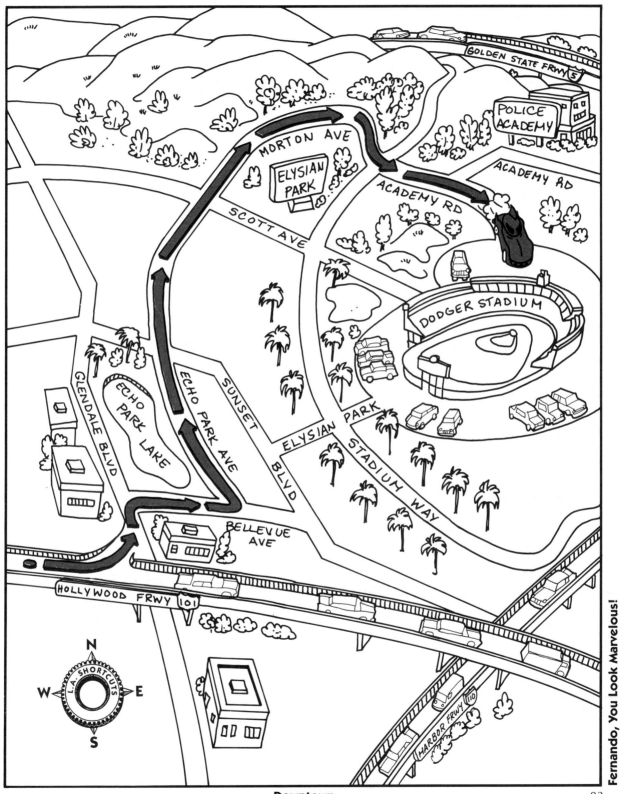

Follow the Silverbrick Road

(Silverlake to Downtown)

THE SCOOP

You've just closed escrow on your two bedroom fixer-upper in Silverlake, one of the last bargain neighborhoods in L.A. The movers have left, the last box is unpacked, and it's time to relax. Suddenly, a thought sends shock waves through the Italian leather couch on which you sit — now you've got to make that horrible haul to your Downtown office every day from Silverlake! Though it's just a few miles, the drive in freeway traffic makes the Civic Center seem like it's located at the end of the earth. Not to worry. Relax once more, because the *Silverbrick Road* will put Downtown back within easy reach.

THE ROUTE

Eastbound on Sunset Blvd., turn south on Park Ave. Turn south again on Glendale Blvd. and continue to 1st St. Go east on 1st and take your last good breath before entering the Civic Center.

BEST HOURS/DIRECTION

This route is most efficient going into Downtown, especially during rush hour.

TIPS

Traffic may back up a bit at Temple, but plow on. Watch carefully for the 1st St. sign as you approach Beverly Blvd. It's a hard left up an on-ramp that's easily missed.

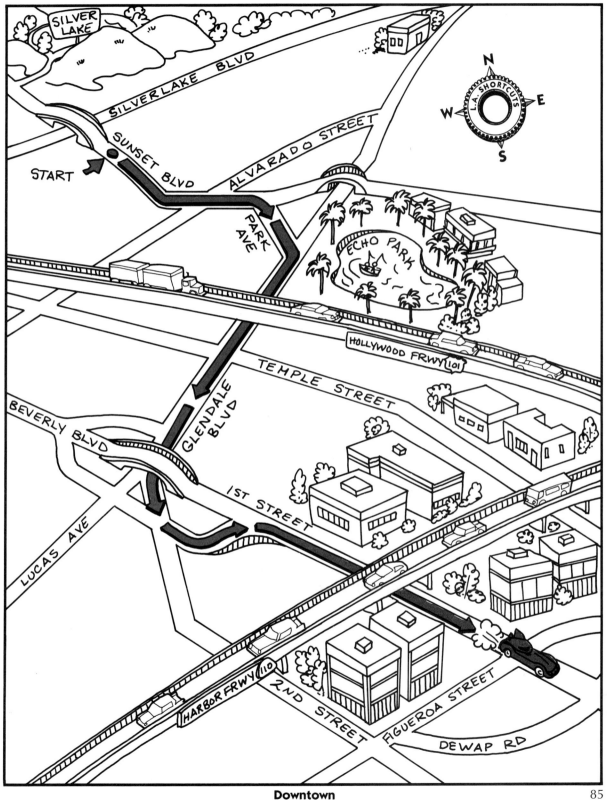

Follow the Silverbrick Road

Fourth and Goal to Go

(Eastbound Downtown Thoroughfare)

SHORTCUT TIME:
4 minutes

T. GUIDE PAGE:
44

THE SCOOP

In the early 60's city planners decided once and for all to revitalize the Downtown area. They settled on a flawless blueprint for the future. Downtown would become a mixed-use area full of condos, upscale markets and high-rises guaranteed to suck residents back to the vicinity. Their efforts were praised as a success, and today the Bunker Hill area indeed is densely populated. But we think their state-of-the-art plan really created a complete state-of-confusion. Innocent motorists get stuck in a labyrinth of multi-level roads leading to and from nowhere. Fortunately, 4th St. remains as a relatively unscathed memorial to a bygone era.

THE ROUTE

Northbound or southbound on the Harbor Freeway, get off at 4th St. It's an eastbound one-way, so you can pass through the Downtown crunch with a minimum wait on the way to your destination.

BEST HOURS/DIRECTION

Though 4th St. has its share of peak-hour traffic, it's a one-way ticket that nearly always out-performs both 1st and 2nd Streets.

TIPS

The farther east you go, the funkier it gets — but you'll soon be rewarded with a plethora of tacky discount toy shops that make Pic 'n' Save look like Neiman Marcus. For you L.A. natives we suggest a quick lesson in the New York Weave — strategically whipping your vehicle from curb to curb to avoid lane blockage.

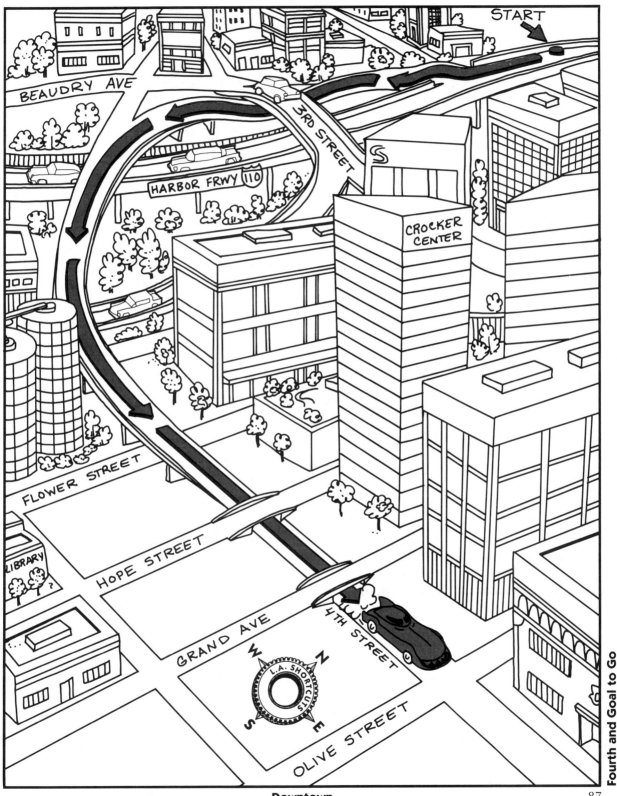

START

BEAUDRY AVE

3RD STREET

HARBOR FRWY 110

CROCKER CENTER

FLOWER STREET

HOPE STREET

LIBRARY

GRAND AVE

4TH STREET

OLIVE STREET

L.A. SHORTCUTS

W N E S

Downtown

87

Fourth and Goal to Go

Hig's Favorite Fig
(Harbor Freeway Alternate)

SHORTCUT TIME:
7 minutes

T. GUIDE PAGES:
44, 52

THE SCOOP

It's ironic that a former Caltrans official, Hig, would abandon the Harbor Freeway in favor of a side street for his daily commute between Long Beach and Downtown. It's a long drive through some rough territory (Compton, Watts, and Willowbrook) so it must be good. We agree with Hig that Figueroa is worth it. Though we can't endorse taking this route as far as Hig prefers, as a parallel to the Harbor Plagueway, it's an enticing alternative.

THE ROUTE

Southbound from the Downtown area, hop onto Figueroa St. and follow it as far as you dare.

BEST HOURS/DIRECTION

This route was timed between Pico and Slauson at rush hour and it cooked. It's great in either direction any time the Harbor Freeway is backed up.

TIPS

Baby-boomers will experience a wave of nostalgia as they pass the giant Felix the Cat sign at Jefferson. For those who tool around in expensive European sedans, we recommend suffering the freeway south of Slauson. *Warning*: do not attempt Figueroa during any event at the Big Four: the Coliseum, Sports Arena, USC, or the Shrine Auditorium.

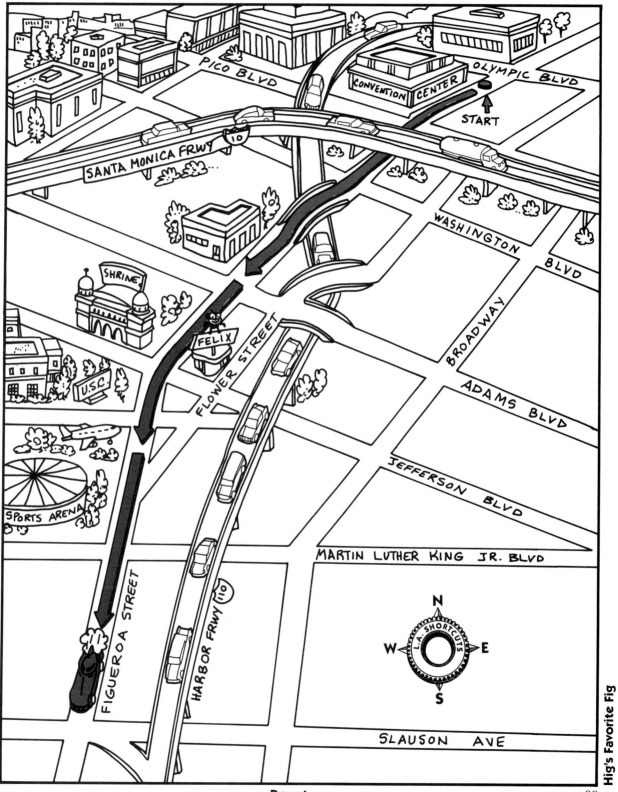

Hill Street Cruise
(Harbor/Pasadena Freeway Downtown Bypass)

THE SCOOP

This shortcut is dedicated to the episode of *"Hill St. Blues"* which thrust shortcuts into the national limelight. In it, two officers made a bet over the quickest route to their precinct. No victor emerged and their wager degenerated into a brawl. But that was TV; this is real life. *Hill St. Cruise* will cure your driving blues when you're cuffed to the Hollywood Freeway and held without bail.

THE ROUTE

Southbound on the Pasadena Freeway, bail out at the Hill St. exit in Chinatown. Laugh at the Metalheads bottled up on the freeway as you slip into Downtown through the side door.

BEST HOURS/DIRECTION

This route works best going towards Downtown during rush hour.

TIPS

Make sure you've got a full stomach when passing through Chinatown or you might be forced to pull over for a bean curd puff pastry. True connoisseurs will jump at the opportunity to dine at that bastion of Chinese cuisine, The Velvet Turtle. (The home of Velvet Turtle Soup?) Just past Sunset, check out the awe-inspiring view of City Hall. And don't forget to miss that uninspiring architectural gem, the D.W.P. fountain.

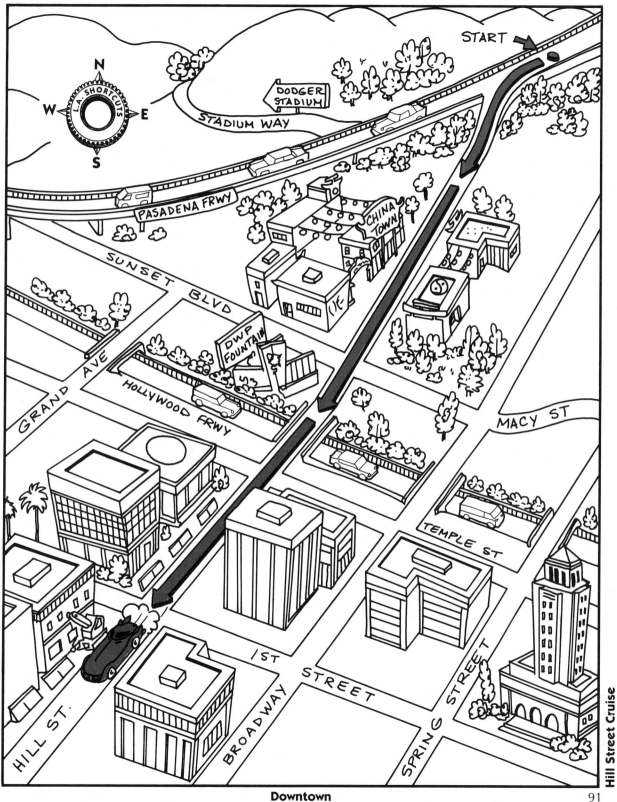

START

N
W — E
S

L.A. SHORTCUTS

DODGER STADIUM

STADIUM WAY

PASADENA FRWY

CHINA TOWN

SUNSET BLVD

GRAND AVE

DWP FOUNTAIN

HOLLYWOOD FRWY

MACY ST

TEMPLE ST

1ST STREET

BROADWAY

SPRING STREET

HILL ST.

Hill Street Cruise

Into the Shrine

(Back Door into the Shrine Auditorium)

SHORTCUT TIME:
3 minutes

T. GUIDE PAGE:
44

THE SCOOP

Los Angeles is one of the great entertainment capitals of the world. On any given day, superstars ranging from the Boss to the Boston Pops perform at a number of excellent venues. Sadly, you are usually accompanied to these intimate affairs by 50,000 unruly, parking-hungry fanatics. When this happens, normally quiet surface streets turn instantly lawless. (Well, you wanted to party!) If your destination is the Shrine Auditorium, you and your friends can still do just that — by going *Into The Shrine* and avoiding the skirmishing multitudes.

THE ROUTE

Eastbound on the Santa Monica Freeway, get off at Hoover St. and go south. At Adams Blvd. veer left and go two blocks before turning south on Severance St. Go east on 28th St. when Severance ends. Follow 28th to University Ave. Turn south on University for one block and then go east on 30th St. Two short blocks later, go south on Shrine Pl. and you'll be at the back door to the Shrine before the opening act takes the stage.

BEST HOURS/DIRECTION

This event-oriented shortcut is great any time you're on your way in and out of the Shrine.

TIPS

Frat brats have been known to remove the Shrine Pl. street sign, so just remember it's right after Royal St. and you'll be OK. Which reminds us: You might want to spend a few of those extra minutes you save with this shortcut taking in the sights as you pass USC's Sorority and Fraternity rows.

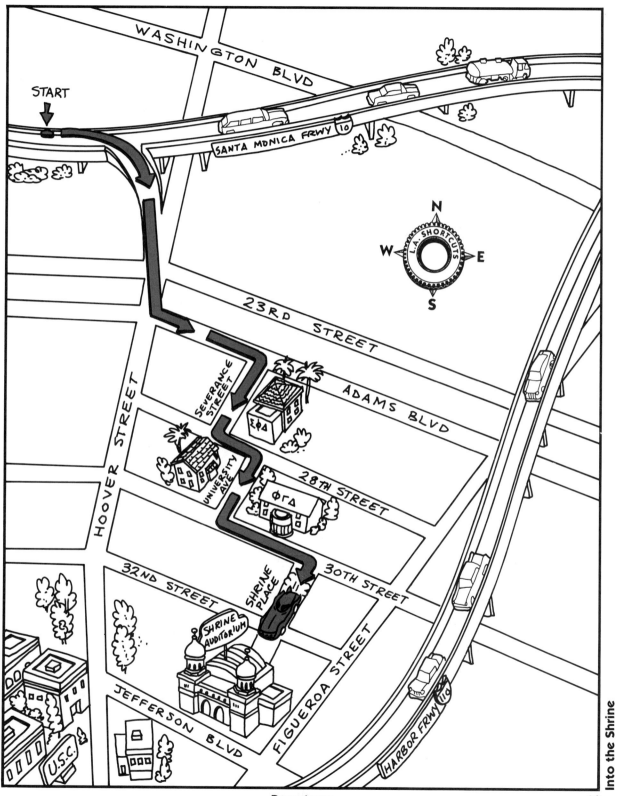

START

WASHINGTON BLVD

SANTA MONICA FRWY 10

N
W E
S
L.A. SHORTCUTS

23RD STREET

ADAMS BLVD

HOOVER STREET

SEVERANCE STREET

ΣΦΔ

UNIVERSITY AVE

ΦΓΔ

28TH STREET

30TH STREET

32ND STREET

SHRINE PLACE

FIGUEROA STREET

SHRINE AUDITORIUM

JEFFERSON BLVD

U.S.C.

HARBOR FRWY 110

Into the Shrine

The Pack Buster

(Santa Monica/Harbor Freeway Interchange Bypass)

SHORTCUT TIME:
7 minutes

T. GUIDE PAGES:
43, 51, 52

THE SCOOP

What are you going to do when you're on a collision course with the snarly cloverleaf of the Santa Monica and Harbor Plagueways? What can you turn to for help? *The Pack Buster.* Lopping off that ghastly interchange in two swift strokes, this shortcut is quick and dirty — literally. Once again you'll find yourself in a rough part of town, but what's a little taste of danger compared to making great time?

THE ROUTE

Eastbound on the Santa Monica Freeway, get off at Vermont Ave. and go south. Take Vermont for about two miles until you get to Vernon Ave. Turn west on Vernon and slide onto the Harbor Freeway southbound.

BEST HOURS/DIRECTION

It's a master blaster in either direction when the freeways are clogged. Since the Pack Buster runs close to the Coliseum, don't attempt to run this gauntlet during sporting or special events.

TIPS

Vernon Ave. is a single lane except from 4:00 to 6:00 p.m., which means this is a great practice field for the New York Weave. Vermont is the original spawning ground for schools of Reckless Traveling Disasters (RTD busses), so stay out of the exhaust-infested right-hand lanes.

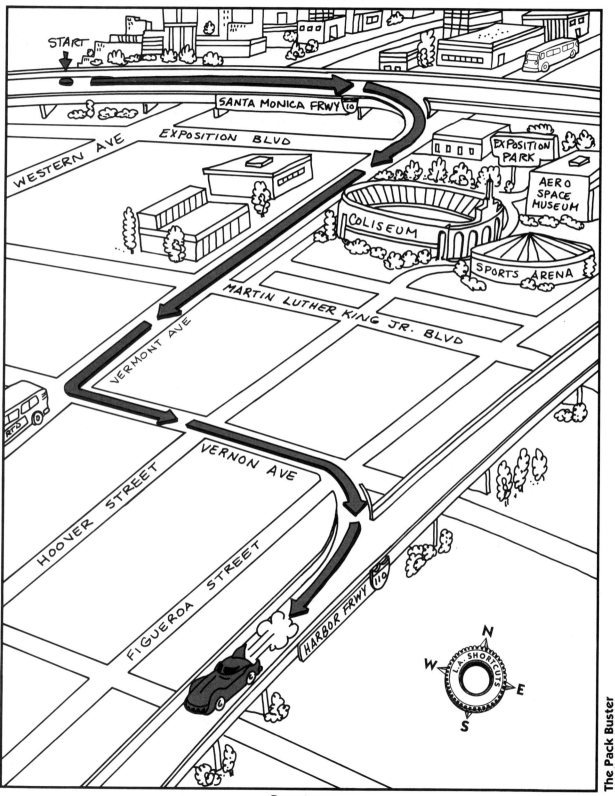

The Pack Buster

The Rampart Bypass
(Harbor/Hollywood Freeway Bypass Out of Downtown)

SHORTCUT TIME:
7 minutes

T. GUIDE PAGES:
35, 44

THE SCOOP
Getting out of Downtown at peak rush hour is about as fun as wolfing down a bag of salted peanuts just after gum surgery. But before you blow your Botts Dots, we've got a route that will get you home quicker than foreign developers can build another corner mini-mall. *The Rampart Bypass* is aptly named, because you'll skirt the daily Harbor/Hollywood fenderfest. This four-star detour will snake you through an area chock-full of nail salons, low-rent hotels, and multi-ethnic fast food joints.

THE ROUTE
Head west on the one-way 8th St., pass over the Harbor Freeway and proceed to Hoover St. Make a right on Hoover and instantly veer right again onto Rampart Blvd. Take Rampart for about a mile until you get to the Hollywood Freeway on-ramp.

BEST HOURS/DIRECTION
You'll get maximum results during rush hour, but *The Rampart Bypass* is great any time. Use it in either direction between both freeways, even though 8th St. turns one-way east of the Harbor Freeway.

TIPS
Westbound, when you turn onto Hoover, make an instant hairpin right turn onto Rampart. It's easy to miss, though, and if this happens you can make a quick right on 7th St. to pick up Rampart again. Things clog up a bit at Wilshire Blvd., but it's definitely worth the short wait. Burger fans will lick their chops when they reach the intersection of Beverly and Rampart, for there lies the original Tommy's Burgers.

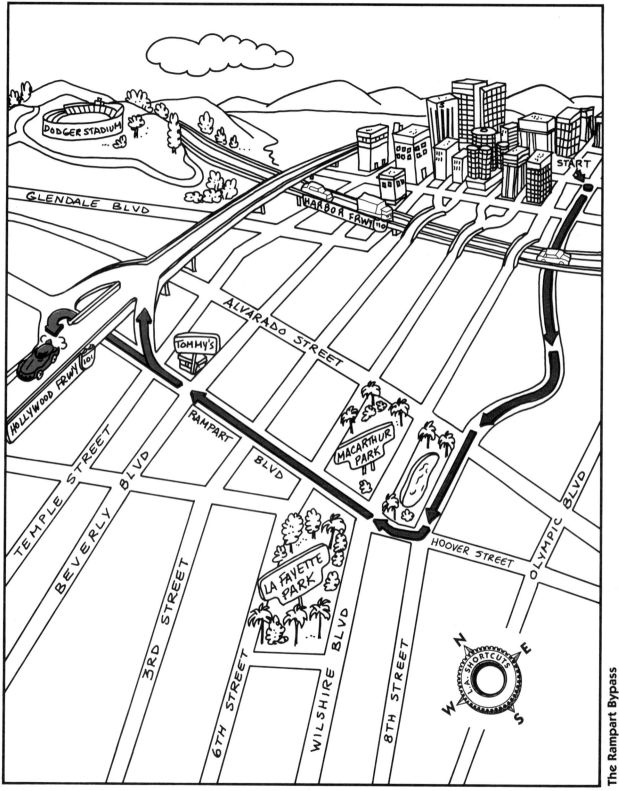

The Rampart Bypass

The 6th Street City Shuffle
(Hollywood to Downtown)

SHORTCUT TIME:
10 minutes

T. GUIDE PAGES:
42, 43, 44

THE SCOOP
In the year 1895, H. Gaylord Wilshire dreamed of building a multi-lane, modern roadway through the heart of Los Angeles. He never lived to see it fully completed, but Wilshire Blvd. became the "pipeline of commerce" he'd always envisioned. Unfortunately, old Gaylord's pipeline was a little too successful. Some unnamed soul outsmarted Wilshire by building a lightning-fast alternate just one block north. It's our belief that if Mr. Wilshire needed to get Downtown today, he'd be driving 6th St., just as we do. Though it's not nearly as long or wide as Wilshire, it will get you to the heart of Downtown quickly — and it's traveled by half as many cars.

THE ROUTE
Starting anywhere on 6th St. east of La Cienega, go east until you see the Bonaventure Hotel. It's the one that looks like it needs a launching pad.

BEST HOURS/DIRECTION
6th St. consistently beats Wilshire, 3rd St., or Beverly Blvd. going anywhere, any time.

TIPS
Beware of the dim-witted Lefties ignoring the "No Left Turn" signs at every major intersection. You'll encounter numerous stop lights between Western and Figueroa, but treat them as little more than eye candy because they'll have no effect on your overall travel time. With a little practice, you'll be doing *The 6th Street City Shuffle* while praising Mr. Wilshire for providing The Pack with a nice, wide resting place.

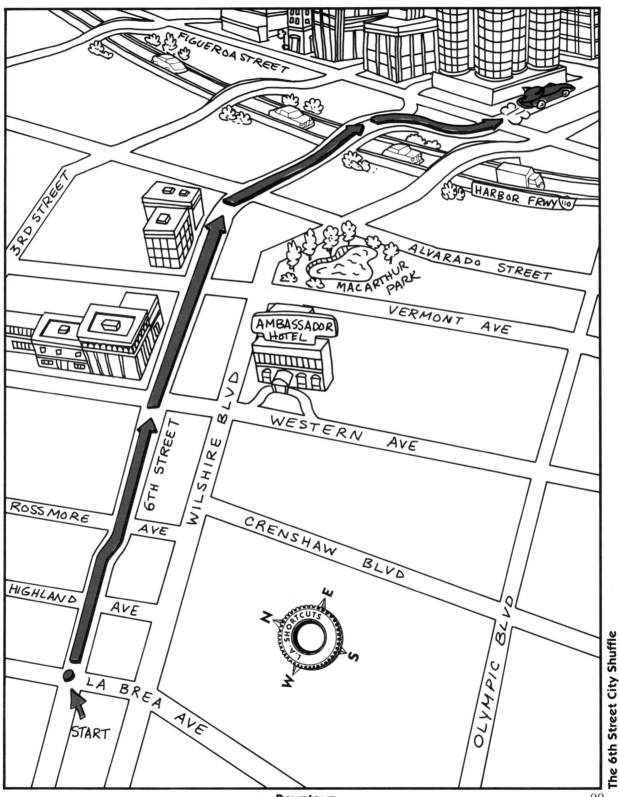

FIGUEROA STREET

3RD STREET

HARBOR FRWY 110

ALVARADO STREET

MACARTHUR PARK

VERMONT AVE

AMBASSADOR HOTEL

WESTERN AVE

6TH STREET

WILSHIRE BLVD

ROSSMORE AVE

CRENSHAW BLVD

HIGHLAND AVE

OLYMPIC BLVD

LA SHORTCUTS

N E S W

LA BREA AVE

START

U-Needa Alameda
(North/South Downtown Artery)

SHORTCUT TIME:
8 minutes

T. GUIDE PAGE:
44

THE SCOOP
Most people would rather suck razor blades than face the grim task of cutting a north/south swath across the Downtown grid. Let's examine the possibilities: Olive is the pits, Flower is wilted, Hope is despairing, and Grand isn't very. *U-Needa Alameda!* It may be gritty and untamed to some, but to Shortcut Sharks, it's a lush oasis between the Hollywood and Santa Monica Plagueways.

THE ROUTE
Easily accessible from both the Hollywood and Santa Monica Freeways east of the Harbor Freeway, Alameda St. is the route to take for all points north or south.

BEST HOURS/DIRECTION
24 hours a day in either direction.

TIPS
Alameda is to the truck driver what Cape Canaveral is to the astronaut: a launch pad for precious payloads. If you eat it or use it, chances are it got to you via Alameda. We mention this because you need to be careful on Alameda, for it's the world's only moving truck stop. And if the trucks don't get you, the train tracks running through the center of the road just might. It's a rough ride, but you'll get to sample some of L.A.'s classic institutions: the Atomic Cafe, the Little Tokyo Bowl, and the Produce Market.

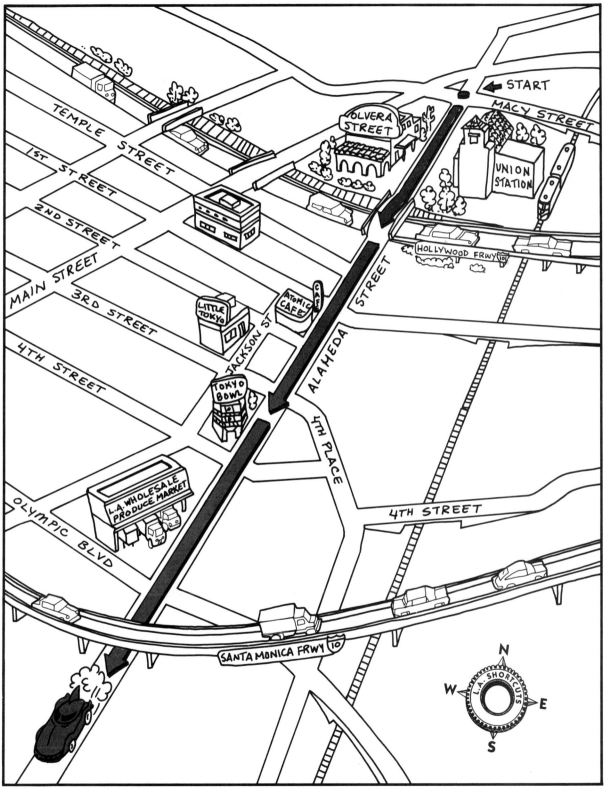

U-Needa Alameda

The Westsider's Sprint to the Games

(Westside Route to the Coliseum)

SHORTCUT TIME:
23 minutes

T. GUIDE PAGES:
42, 43, 51

THE SCOOP

The folks at Caltrans fondly look back upon the 1984 Summer Games as the golden days of free-flowing freeways. Going to the Coliseum? No problem. Too bad it didn't last. Today you're likely to experience the first quarter of the Raiders game stuck in bumper-to-bumper traffic a mile from the Exposition off-ramp while grinding your teeth to the play-by-play. But why be held for no gain? We've got an end sweep that will get Westsiders to the Coliseum/Sports Arena with plenty of time to scalp their extra tickets.

THE ROUTE

Take Robertson Blvd. south until it turns into Higuera St. at Washington Blvd. At La Cienega, Higuera St. turns into Rodeo Rd. (pronounced ROH-dee-oh, unlike its Beverly Hills counterpart). Follow Rodeo all the way to Budlong Ave. and turn south. At Martin Luther King, Jr. Blvd, turn east, go three blocks and start looking for a parking space.

BEST HOURS/DIRECTION

This route scores big during any major sporting event at the Coliseum or Sports Arena. You can use it either direction. It's also a great way to get in and out of Downtown.

TIPS

Take the pedal off the metal around the home stretch on Rodeo Rd. — this mini freeway attracts our friends in blue like a House of Pies. Rodeo serves double-duty as an excellent east/west relief-valve for the Santa Monica Plagueway.

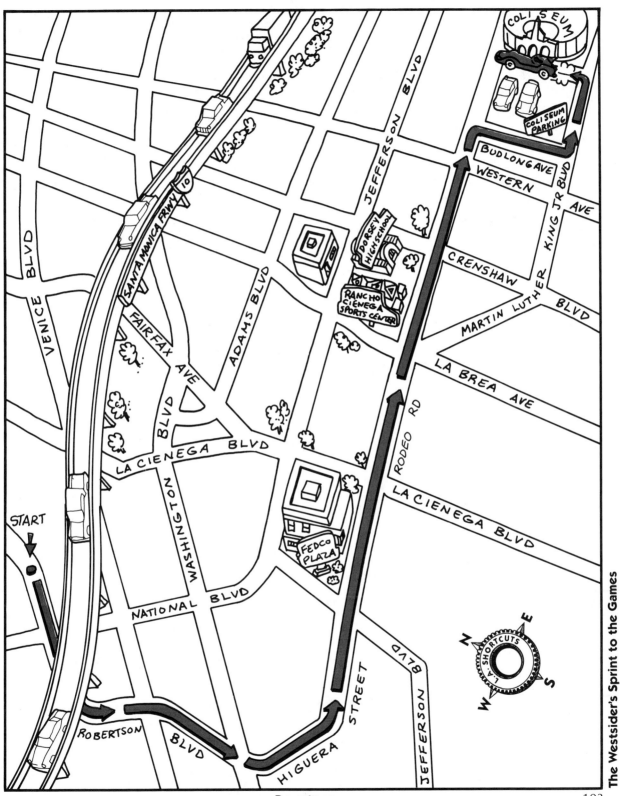

The Westsider's Sprint to the Games

Hollywood

Hollywood is the quintessential commuter's town. A flock-and-flee place where millions want to work but few want to live. It's a familiar scene... young Turks toil to create "entertainment," only to trundle their hefty paychecks off to the creature comforts of the Westside. What's left is a seedy underbelly, mean streets of fast living and slow traffic. Sadly, the landmarks of the dream that once lured millions to Tinseltown are being bulldozed for yet another corner mini-mall.

Road travel in Hollywood is a life-threatening endeavor. Tourists, cruisers, and cops make nighttime driving a horror show. To make matters worse, nearly every major street in Hollywood begins and ends outside the city limits, adding hordes of cross-towners to the already clogged picture. For Shortcut Sharks this means driving our parallel, short-range alternate routes.

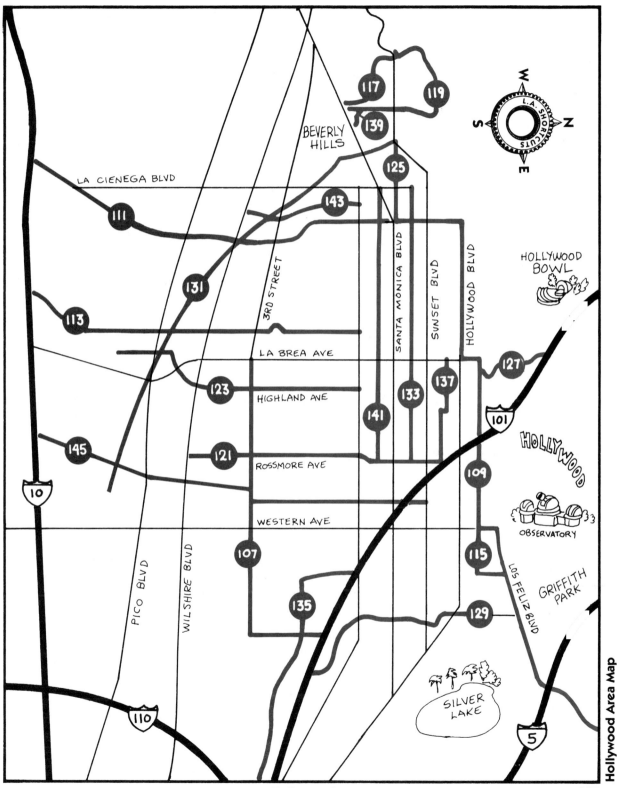

Hollywood Area Map

A Constant Virgil

(North/South Vermont Alternate into East Hollywood)

SHORTCUT TIME:
6 minutes

T. GUIDE PAGE:
34

THE SCOOP

It's a sweltering Hollywood afternoon — the perfect setting for a third-rate romance and low-rent rendezvous. Heading north in your late-model Bonneville, all traffic suddenly stops as the streets turn into flypaper. It's a standard Hollywood tune sung by those doomed to travel the dark, seedy corridors known as Vermont and Western Avenues. In a hot flash, your carnal desires quickly turn into wilted flowers and melted chocolates. Looking to your plastic dashboard demigod for guidance, you'll notice its holy hand pointing the way to salvation — Virgil Ave.

THE ROUTE

Starting near La Brea and 3rd St., follow 3rd past Vermont to Virgil Ave. Turn north on Virgil and accelerate your way into the sanctified regions of East Hollywood.

BEST HOURS/DIRECTION

Virgil is great most of the time but you'll find some resistance during the morning rush hours heading south.

TIPS

At Sunset and Virgil you'll hit an awkward intersection that causes blue-haired ladies to panic at the pedals. Ignore it and press on to the next one at Temple and Silver-lake. If you're brave and hardy, stop in for a quick burrito at one of the tiny Mexican fast-food joints along the way.

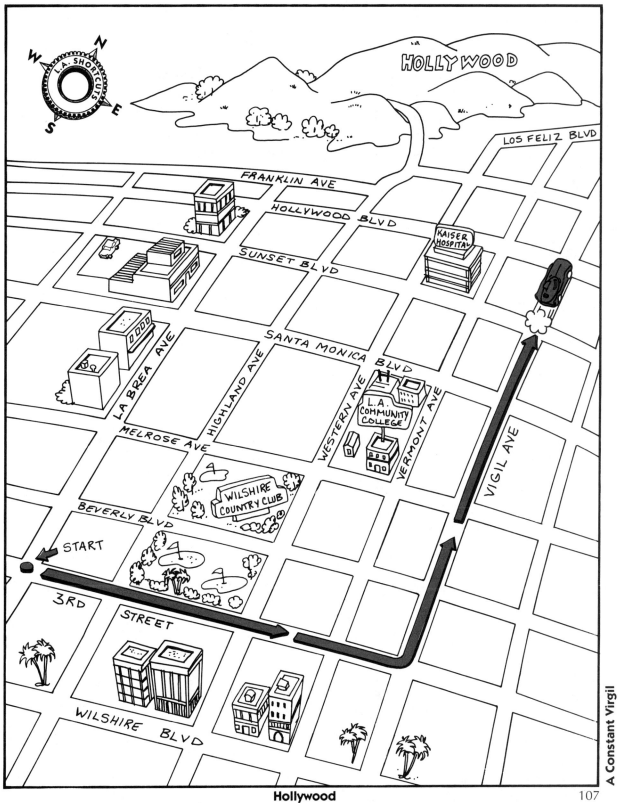

Hollywood

A Constant Virgil

Brian's Stepladder Across Hollywood

(East/West Sweep Across Hollywood)

SHORTCUT TIME: T. GUIDE PAGES:
12 minutes   33, 34

THE SCOOP

D.W. Griffith once directed a movie called *"Intolerance."* This word aptly describes what it's like trying to go east or west across Hollywood on any of the major boulevards: Hollywood, Sunset, or Santa Monica. These streets will never be nominated for a best-supporting role in getting you anywhere, any time. So if you're in a rush to close that big deal, use our Academy Award-winning alternate. And the next time someone mentions Sunset Blvd., tell them it's a great movie but a lousy street.

ROUTE

Westbound from Vermont Ave., take Franklin Ave. to Highland Ave. Make sure you nose up to the intersection in the left-hand lane. Go south on Highland for one block and turn west on the continuation of Franklin. At La Brea Ave. go south to Hollywood Blvd. and turn west. (Don't worry, there's no traffic on this stretch.) Cruise Hollywood Blvd. past the big line of cars making a left turn at Fairfax and proceed to Laurel Ave. Go south on Laurel (See why it's named the "stepladder"?) to Fountain Ave. and turn west. Continue to La Cienega and your destination — though we'd stop for a beer at Barney's Beanery.

BEST HOURS/DIRECTION

You're going to get the top performance from this route during the morning rush hour in either direction. Eastbound in the evening rush is slow going at Gower St., otherwise this shortcut is great at any time of day.

TIPS

Going westbound in the evening, watch out for the thundering herd stampeding its way towards the freeway at Argyle Ave. and Franklin. Try to dash past the intersection of Franklin and Highland Ave. Remember that just three blocks south is the seventh most-traveled intersection in the city (Sunset and Highland), handling

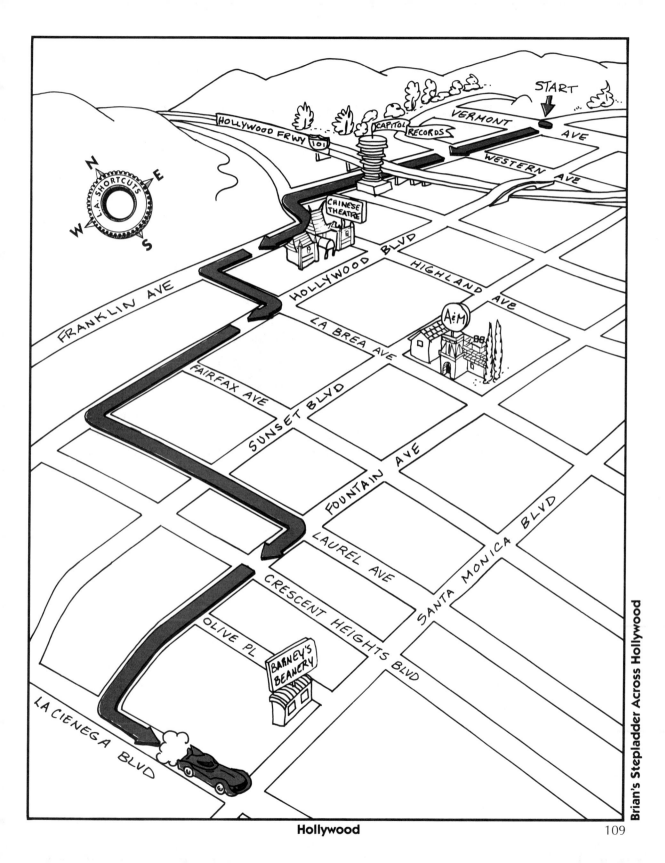

START

VERMONT AVE

WESTERN AVE

HOLLYWOOD FRWY 101

CAPITOL RECORDS

CHINESE THEATRE

N
E
W
S
L.A. SHORTCUTS

FRANKLIN AVE

HOLLYWOOD BLVD

HIGHLAND AVE

LA BREA AVE

A&M

FAIRFAX AVE

SUNSET BLVD

FOUNTAIN AVE

SANTA MONICA BLVD

LAUREL AVE

CRESCENT HEIGHTS BLVD

OLIVE PL

BARNEY'S BEANERY

LA CIENEGA BLVD

Brian's Stepladder Across Hollywood

Crescent Heights Delight
(North/South La Cienega Bypass into Hollywood)

SHORTCUT TIME: **T. GUIDE PAGES:**
  9 minutes   42, 33

THE SCOOP
Here's a time-honored standby of all veteran Shortcut Sharks. Granted, Crescent Heights isn't what it used to be, but it's still a cannon blast compared to the pea shot up La Cienega. It's a class act all the way, especially between Pico and Olympic Blvds., where you pass a stretch of vintage California Spanish-style duplexes built in the 1930s. Cut back on the gas if you want a better look; otherwise everything will be a blur.

THE ROUTE
Northbound on La Cienega Blvd. in the vicinity of the Santa Monica Freeway, turn east on Guthrie Ave. just past Kaiser Permanente Hospital. Go one block and turn north on Crescent Heights Blvd. From there it's an easy cruise all the way up to Sunset Blvd.

BEST HOURS/DIRECTION
You'll get maximum performance northbound during the morning rush. Southbound in the evening can get a bit ugly at the major intersections north of Wilshire — a true test of driving skills for those who love a challenge.

TIPS
Crescent Heights is chock-full of the worst kinds of drivers. You'll pass Slomofos, Lefties, Oliveheads, and all other species of road hogs. To make good time you must weave to and fro, right and left, to gain yardage. Before approaching San Vicente, get in the right lane. Otherwise you'll sit and watch three green lights go by. Beginning south of Airdrome you'll encounter a group of four-way stops that are more fun than a long, wet kiss on a slow Ferris wheel.

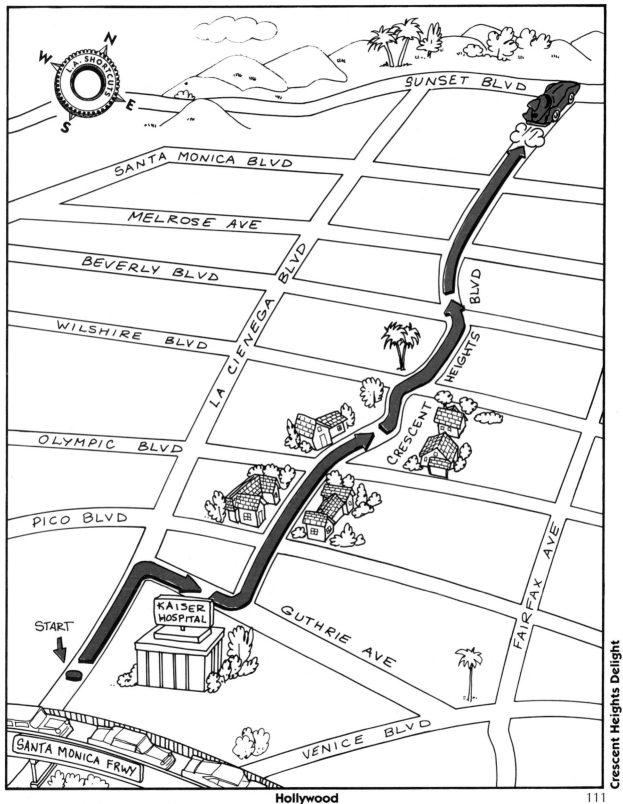

Crescent Heights Delight

Doin' the Hauser Hop to Hancock Park

(North/South La Brea Alternate into Hollywood)

SHORTCUT TIME:
5 minutes

T. GUIDE PAGES:
34, 42, 43

THE SCOOP

The war is over for the brave warriors who use Fairfax Ave. in their crusade into Hancock Park. Put away those grenades you saved for blasting through the Cadillacs and Cordobas on Fairfax and La Brea. Introducing the "peacekeeper" — Hauser Blvd. — a strategic, short-range urban assault corridor. Had Reagan brandished a "Hauser" at the Moscow summit, *Star Wars* " might now be remembered as just another classic film.

THE ROUTE

From the Santa Monica Freeway going either direction, get off at Washington Blvd./ Fairfax and turn east on Washington Blvd. Turn north at Hauser Blvd. and push, pump, and pound those pedals to 3rd St. (You're now doing the "hop.") At 3rd St.... presto! Hauser turns into Martel Ave., where you're back on your own. If you must fight your way farther north, follow Martel as long as your courage holds out.

BEST HOURS/DIRECTION

This route is available 24 hours a day with maximum results.

TIPS

When approaching any major east/west intersection, be sure to thread your way into the right-hand lane to avoid the Lefties. Southbound in the evening, Hauser tends to back up between Pico and Venice Blvds., but hang in there. Between 3rd St. and 6th St. is L.A.'s own Bermuda Triangle: The Park La Brea Maze. People have been known to mysteriously vanish there. Keep your head down, and whatever you do, don't stop for directions.

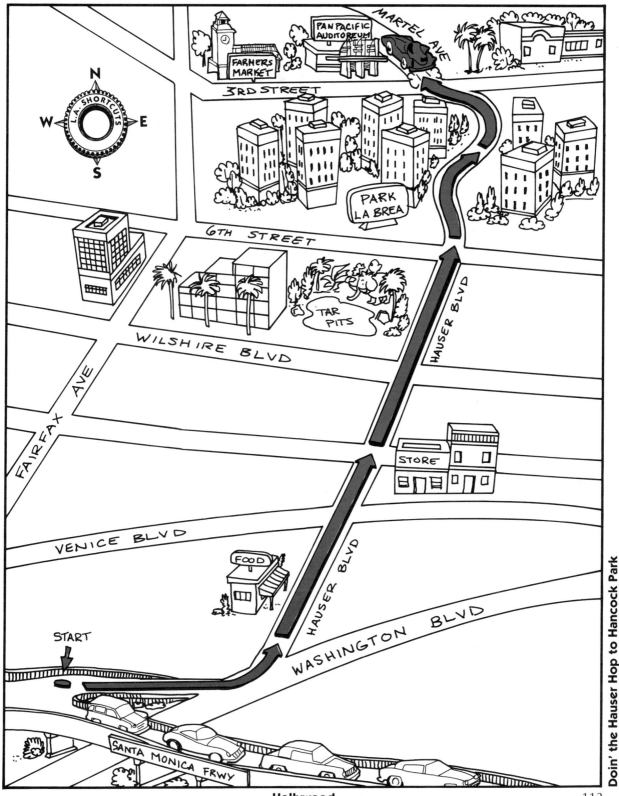

Doin' the Hauser Hop to Hancock Park

Failsafe to Glendale

(Hollywood to Glendale)

SHORTCUT TIME:
8 minutes

T. GUIDE PAGES:
25, 34, 35

THE SCOOP

Los Feliz is one of the few neighborhoods that has miraculously managed to retain its character throughout the years. The Beverly Hills of its day, this area attracted new-money moguls who built boulevards wide enough to cruise their Dusenbergs in style. In time, the new money became old money. The luxury cruisers shrank into fuel-efficient shoe boxes. Yet the broad boulevards remained. For this reason, we hereby dub Los Feliz Blvd. a four-star stretch between Hollywood and Glendale.

THE ROUTE

Eastbound on Franklin Ave., go past Western Ave. to Serrano Ave. and turn north. Turn east on Los Feliz Blvd. and tool down past the Golden State Freeway, crossing the Los Angeles River until Los Feliz ends at Glendale Ave. Turn north on Glendale and follow it right into beautiful downtown Glendale.

BEST HOURS/DIRECTION

Each morning, Commubots flock down Los Feliz into Hollywood, turning this route into a minor teeth grinder. Luckily, traffic is rarely as bad as it looks. Ditto for eastbound evening travel.

TIPS

Los Lefties drive Los Feliz in droves. If you're not careful you'll get stuck behind one turning onto any of the residential streets between traffic signals. We suggest the New York Weave technique to dodge problem areas, but watch for joggers on the right-hand shoulder. Refresh yourself on hot, summer days by taking a quick dip in the Mulholland Memorial fountain at Riverside Dr.

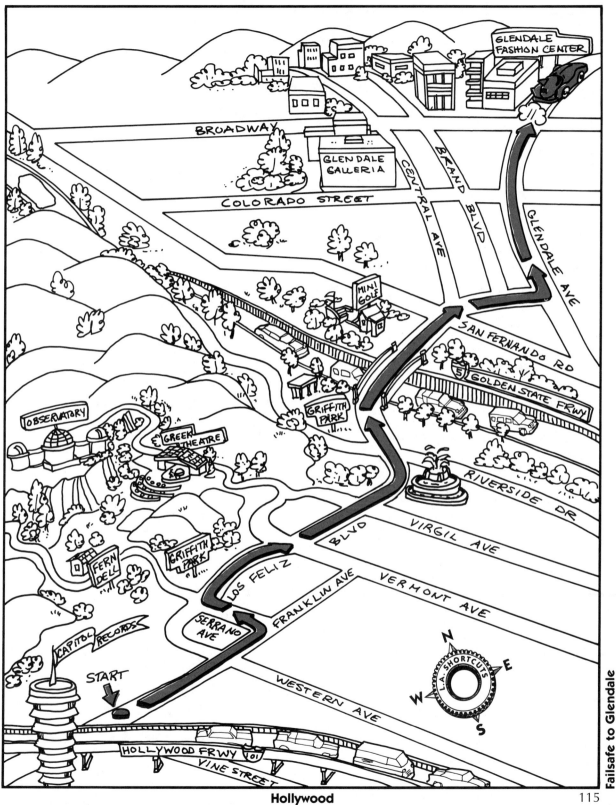

From Strip to Strap
(Short-Range Sunset Strip Detour)

SHORTCUT TIME:
1 minute

T. GUIDE PAGE:
33

THE SCOOP
It used to be a special treat to drive down the Sunset Strip and take in the sideshow. Today, there is no more loathsome experience than being glued to the pavement in what is now a decadent hodgepodge of unglamorous commerce. For this reason, your main objective is to get out of the area as quickly as possible. While it may seem like a small-time detour, *From Strip to Strap* serves up some big drive-time savings.

THE ROUTE
Eastbound on Sunset Blvd. just before the "Strip," turn south into the alley just before the 9200 (Luckman) building. Turn right on Sierra Dr. right behind the building. Go about a block until Sierra turns into Cynthia St. and veer left. Follow Cynthia to Doheny Blvd. and turn south to get to West Hollywood, or plow north to connect back with Sunset.

BEST HOURS/DIRECTION
This is strictly an eastbound detour. Though it's a 24-hour bonanza, the route really pays off during peak rush hours.

TIPS
This shortcut takes a little practice. The alley just west of the 9200 (Luckman) building is easy to miss. Look for the backside of a stop sign for your cue to turn right. You'll be traveling through narrow streets, so don't blow the needle off the speedo.

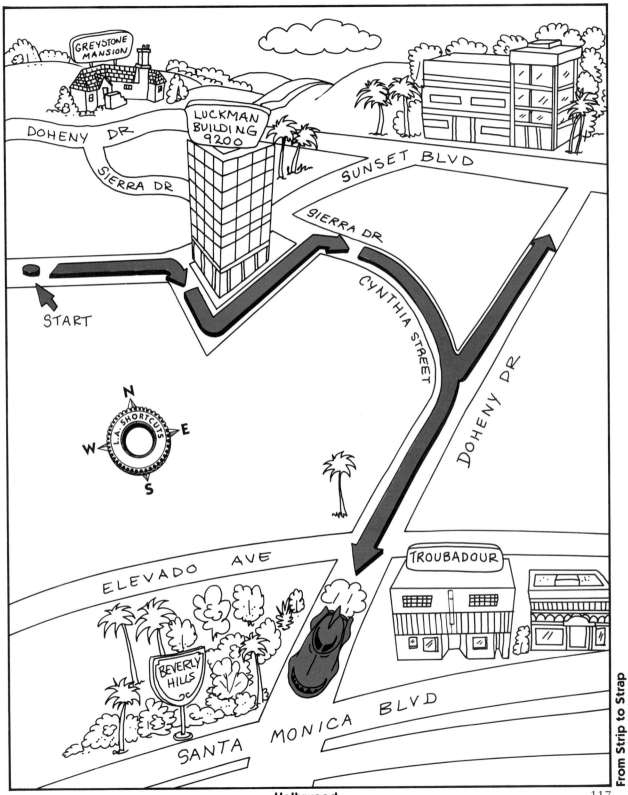

START

GREYSTONE MANSION

LUCKMAN BUILDING 9200

DOHENY DR

SIERRA DR

SUNSET BLVD

SIERRA DR

CYNTHIA STREET

DOHENY DR

N
W E
S

L.A. SHORTCUTS

ELEVADO AVE

BEVERLY HILLS

TROUBADOUR

SANTA MONICA BLVD

From Strip to Strap

Gil Turner's Turnaround

(Short-Range Sunset Blvd. Bypass to West Hollywood)

SHORTCUT TIME:
1 minute

T. GUIDE PAGE:
33

THE SCOOP

Let's say you've just finished the #20 burger (with Jack cheese and spinach) at the Trousdale Hamburger Hamlet and you need to get back to Beverly Hills. As usual, the traffic on Sunset Blvd. is backed up from the Beverly Hills Hotel, so making a U-turn is out of the question. There's only one option left: *Gil Turner's Turnaround*. Though this probably is the shortest of shortcuts, one drive will convince you that less can, indeed, be more.

THE ROUTE

At the Hamburger Hamlet on Doheny Rd. (just off Sunset Blvd.), head north on Sunset Hills Rd. until it curves around and meets upper Doheny Dr. Turn south on Doheny drive and plow down into Beverly Hills or West Hollywood.

BEST HOURS/DIRECTION

This shortcut is great any time when going to Beverly Hills/West Hollywood.

TIPS

Sunset Hills Rd. is steep and winding, but once you reach Doheny, it's a straight shot down the hill to West Hollywood. We highly recommend you stop at least once at Gil Turner's liquor store — one of the few Sunset Strip landmarks that has survived the face lifts of the 80's.

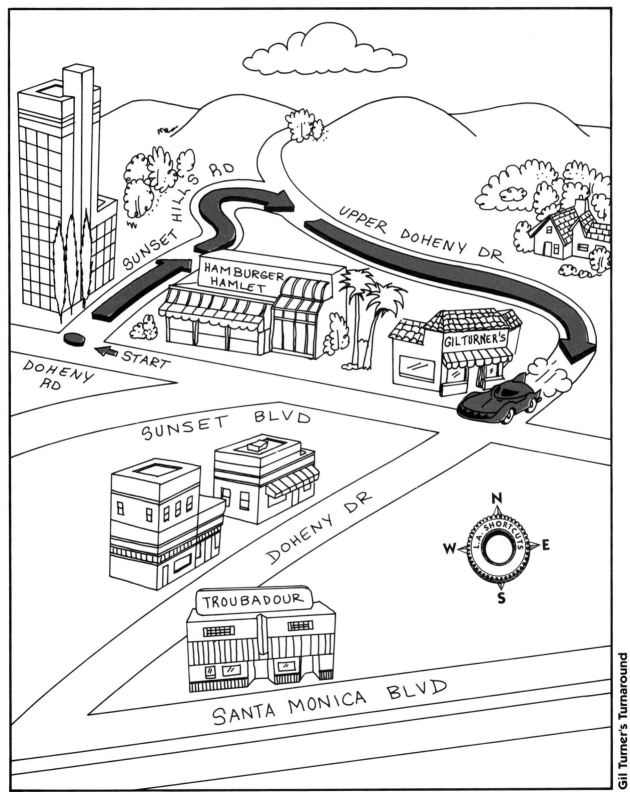

Gil Turner's Turnaround

Herd 'em Through the Grapevine

(North/South Central Hollywood Artery)

T. GUIDE PAGES:
34, 43

SHORTCUT TIME:
6 minutes

THE SCOOP

Stuck on Highland and just about to lose your mind? You've got to "herd it through the Grapevine." Vine St., that is. Whisking you from the exclusive Hancock Park estates into the epicenter of Hollywood's feckless attempt at urban revitalization, we pick Vine St. for the trip into the bleeding heart of Hollywood.

THE ROUTE

From Wilshire Blvd. turn north on Rossmore Ave. and gallop all the way until it turns into Vine St. in Hollywood. Continue on Vine to the sleazy Hollywood destination of your choice.

BEST HOURS/DIRECTION

Going north, the intersection of Melrose Ave. and Rossmore tends to get clogged up at rush hour. Stay to the right to avoid Lefties jockeying for position. Also, at rush hour the section between Hollywood Blvd. and Melrose can bottle up, but the lights are timed well for easy passage.

TIPS

The road narrows between Melrose and 3rd St., so stay to the right and hug the curb to pass slow movers. Be sure to dodge the smoke-spewing Reckless Traveling Disasters (RTD's) that hog both lanes. Architecture buffs won't want to miss the statuesque Hollywood apartments that line Rossmore just south of Melrose.

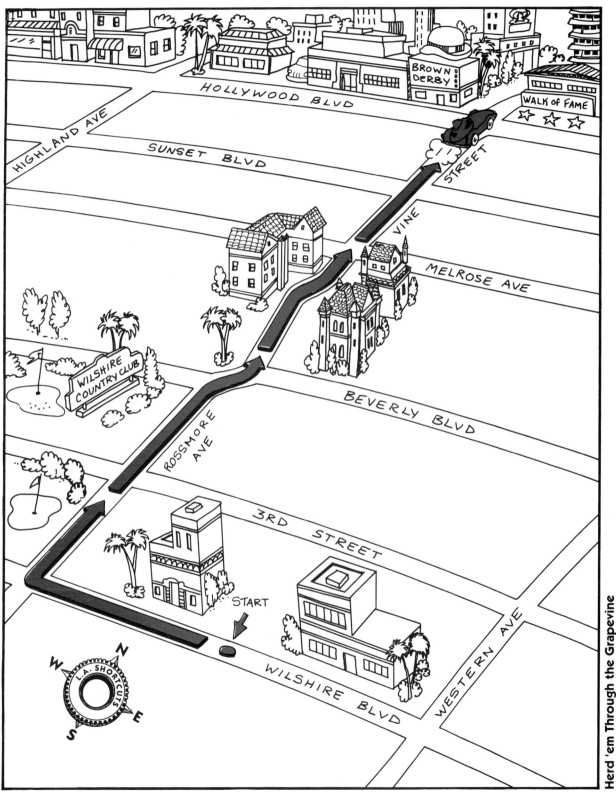

HOLLYWOOD BLVD

HIGHLAND AVE

SUNSET BLVD

BROWN DERBY

WALK OF FAME

VINE STREET

MELROSE AVE

WILSHIRE COUNTRY CLUB

BEVERLY BLVD

ROSSMORE AVE

3RD STREET

START

WESTERN AVE

WILSHIRE BLVD

L.A. SHORTCUTS

W N E S

Herd 'em Through the Grapevine

Highway to Hollywood
(North/South Central Hollywood Artery)

THE SCOOP

The first question most newcomers ask on their inaugural visit to our budding mega-lopolis is, "How do I get to Hollywood?". The enduring popularity of this question sets one wondering why Caltrans didn't acknowledge it when they designed the elaborate freeway system of Los Angeles. Even the novice freeway jockey is confounded by the unforgivable oversight of an expressway into the heart of Hollywood. As a result, it's every driver for himself on Fairfax, La Brea, and La Cienega. You can elude this foray by slipping between the cracks on our *Highway to Hollywood.*

THE ROUTE

From the middle of Hollywood, make your way onto Highland Ave. southbound until you cross Olympic Blvd. One block south of Olympic, Highland turns into Edgewood Pl. Veer right and cross La Brea Ave. Go three blocks and turn south on Redondo Blvd. Rip down Redondo to Venice Blvd. and turn west. Follow Venice to the Santa Monica Freeway, or continue on to the Westside.

BEST HOURS/DIRECTION

Due to the heavy amount of commuter traffic in and out of Hollywood, there's no way to avoid certain slow areas during rush hour in either direction. Melrose, Beverly, and Wilshire are your biggest obstacles. Once you pass them, you're home free.

TIPS

Highland turns into a swift moving "highway" just south of Melrose. But if you're headed north, get off past Melrose. Otherwise you'll hit the Hollywood lookie-loos who will mutilate your schedule. The longest wait will occur at the intersection of Edgewood and La Brea in the late afternoon. Don't sweat it; a look at the madness on La Brea will quickly convince you it's the only way to go.

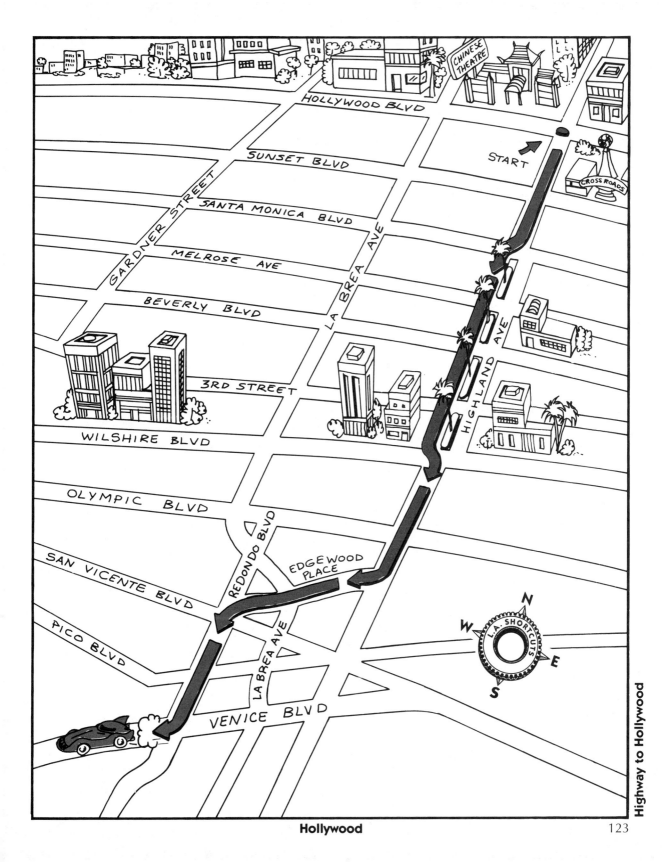

The Hollyvator
(Short-Range Santa Monica to Sunset Blvd. Connector)

SHORTCUT TIME:
1 minute

T. GUIDE PAGE:
33

THE SCOOP
Diehard Shortcut Sharks would never call Holloway Dr. a true shortcut. But since we're writing the book, we stand behind this byway as the only decent trail connecting Santa Monica and Sunset Boulevards in this area.

THE ROUTE
Eastbound on Sunset Blvd., take Holloway Dr. to connect with Santa Monica Blvd.

BEST HOURS/DIRECTION
During non-rush hours it's a breeze. And when faced with the dismal rush hour alternatives, San Vicente and La Cienega, the small crowds on *The Hollyvator* won't seem so bad.

TIPS
For those traveling eastbound on the long haul into Hollywood, don't turn left on La Cienega — just continue on Holloway for two more blocks and turn north on Olive Dr. From there you can pick *Brian's Stepladder Across Hollywood* when you get to Fountain.

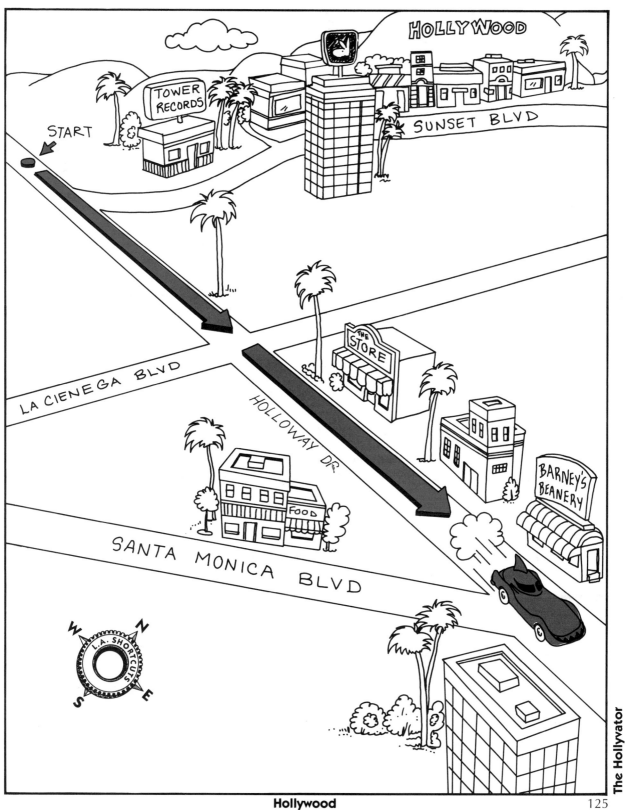

The Hollyvator

Hollywood Bowl Special

(Southern Cahuenga Pass Bail-Out to Hollywood)

SHORTCUT TIME:
6 minutes

T. GUIDE PAGE:
34

THE SCOOP

In a misguided attempt to resurrect the glory days of Tinseltown, the Hollywood Redevelopment Program has transformed Hollywood Blvd. into a public relations circus. Today, any third-rate promoter can abuse the Boulevard for countless cheap, meaningless media events. Parades, Walk of Fame Celebrations, and lame publicity stunts all close down the area and clog every surrounding surface street. For the unfortunate folks trying to go about their daily business, these public masturbations make Dante's *Inferno* seem like a weekend picnic. Though this route runs less than a mile, it will eliminate the hardest mile you'll ever drive.

THE ROUTE

Bail out of the southbound grind on Highland Ave., by turning west on Camrose Dr. near the Hollywood Bowl. Go up the hill and around to the left until Camrose ends at Hillcrest Dr. Turn right on Hillcrest as it curves around to the left and ends at Fitch Dr. Make a right on Fitch and go one block to Sycamore Ave. Go south on Sycamore and make a short dash to Franklin Ave.

BEST HOURS/DIRECTION

During any major event this route is guaranteed to save your sanity as well as your driving time. We recommend using it in heavy morning and evening rush hours when Cahuenga and Franklin are stacked to the max.

TIPS

As soon as you enter the *Hollywood Bowl Special,* you'll be faced with the formidable task of navigating through narrow winding streets, blind curves, and poorly parked cars. The one-way streets surrounding the Yamashiro restaurant create their own concrete version of the California roll. So, when going north use Sycamore (one-way). Heading south, use Fitch (one-way) to the two-way intersection of Sycamore. Confused? We strongly recommend following the map your first time out.

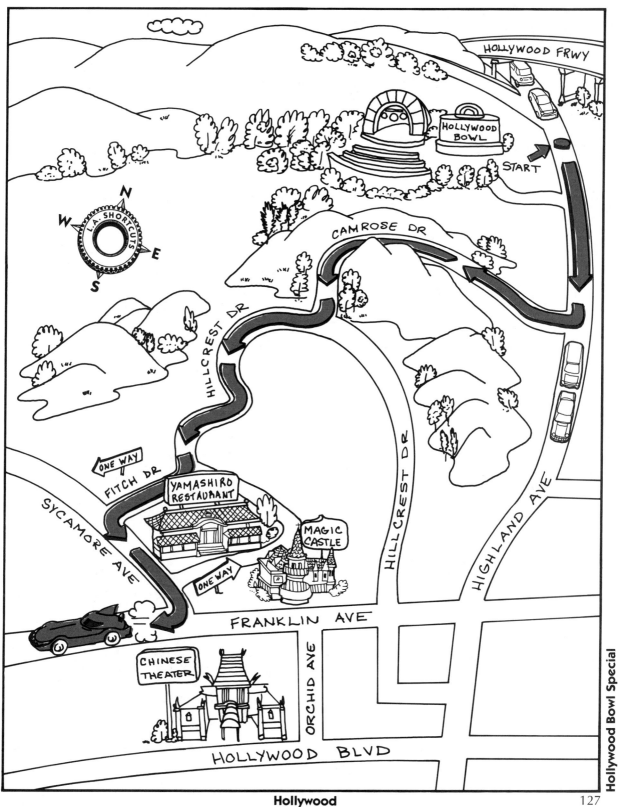

HOLLYWOOD FRWY

HOLLYWOOD BOWL

START

N
W — L.A. SHORTCUTS — E
S

CAMROSE DR

HILLCREST DR

HILLCREST DR

HIGHLAND AVE

ONE WAY

FITCH DR

SYCAMORE AVE

YAMASHIRO RESTAURANT

MAGIC CASTLE

ONE WAY

FRANKLIN AVE

ORCHID AVE

CHINESE THEATER

HOLLYWOOD BLVD

Knoblock's 1-2-3 to ABC
(Hollywood Freeway to ABC Studios)

SHORTCUT TIME:
5 minutes

T. GUIDE PAGE:
35

THE SCOOP

You're a seasoned news hound with Eyewitless News. It's the end of a tough day, and you're knocking back a grilled cheese at the De-Cap Cities/ABC commissary. Suddenly the mojo wire starts to hum with the urgent news of an impromptu bikini contest Downtown. Rookies might whine about making the drek trek to the city center at rush hour. But you've long since incorporated *Knoblock's 1-2-3 to ABC* into your driving repertoire and can wrap up the bare facts in time to return for a slice of pumpkin pie. Even if you're not playing this scene from *Broadcast News,* the *1-2-3* will score high ratings as a scheduled route between Los Feliz and Silverlake.

THE ROUTE

Northbound on the Hollywood Freeway, get off at Silverlake Blvd. Immediately jump into the left-hand lane and turn west on London St. Follow London for two blocks and turn north on Hoover St. Cruise up Hoover for a mile or so until you get to the "V" intersection at Myra St. Turn onto Myra, which does a little jog right and then left as you cross under Sunset Blvd. One block after Sunset, turn west on Effe St. and go one block to Talmadge St. Go north on Talmadge until you face ABC at the corner of Prospect Ave.

BEST HOURS/DIRECTION

24 hours in either direction.

TIPS

Hoover cooks in the residential areas, but crossing the stop sign at Fountain presents a challenge. Keep your eyes peeled for Effe St., as it's easily missed if you're in a hurry. This shortcut can be tough the first time out, but after a few runs you'll see that familiarity breeds speed.

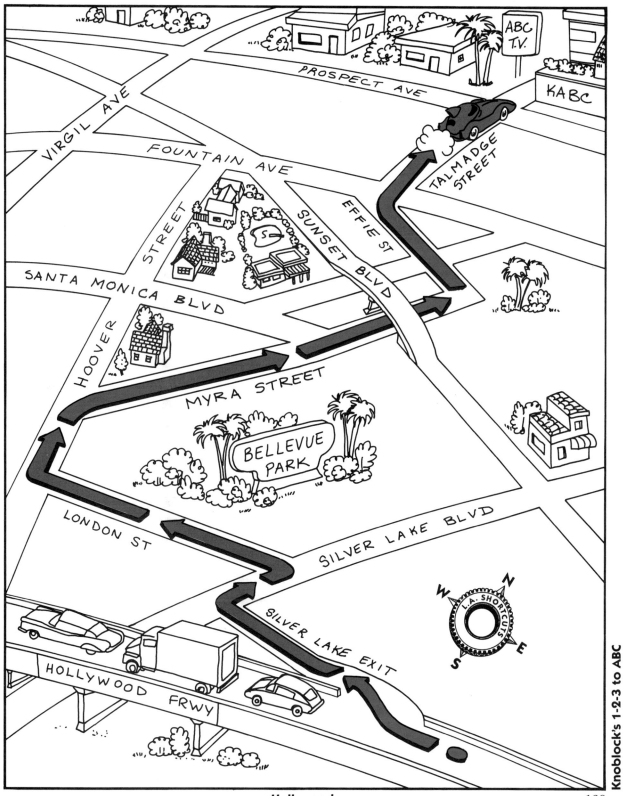

Hollywood

Knoblock's 1-2-3 to ABC

No Jive 45

(West Hollywood To Santa Monica Freeway)

SHORTCUT TIME:
12 minutes

T. GUIDE PAGES:
33, 42, 43

THE SCOOP

Forty-five degrees might be the temperature of a wintery California evening. It could also be the frightening incline of a Mammoth Mountain ski run. But to a driving demon, forty-five degrees is the heavenly angle of San Vicente Blvd. — a roomy road that slashes across a large portion of L.A.'s street grid. It's surprising that urban planners would build such an appropriately angled boulevard — especially since most of the city's streets appear to have been designed by T-square toting flattops.

THE ROUTE

Starting at Sunset Blvd., take San Vicente Blvd. south all the way to Crenshaw Blvd. At Crenshaw you can turn south and go to the Santa Monica Freeway or stay on San Vicente as it turns into Venice Blvd., and go downtown.

BEST HOURS/DIRECTION

Considering the alternatives, this route smokes 24 hours a day in either direction.

TIPS

Feeling hungry <u>and</u> daring? Stop at Johnnies, the famous and funky French-dip pastrami stand on Adams Blvd. near Crenshaw. The neighborhood is wild and the customers drive and park like maniacs. But the sandwiches and the sideshow are both more than worth the trip.

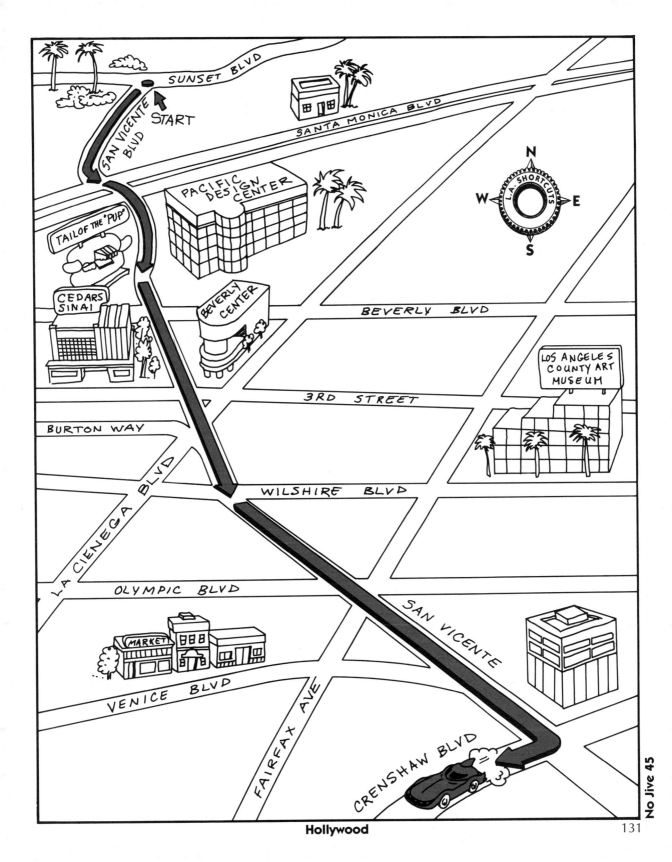

The Old Shortcutter's Trail
(East/West Hollywood/West Hollywood Artery)

SHORTCUT TIME:
10 minutes

T. GUIDE PAGES:
33, 34

THE SCOOP

Inspiration. It's an insatiable urge that eventually leads great people to achieve great things. Dizzie, for example, had the thrill of his first be-bop. Spielberg dreamed Technicolor from the lens of his home movie camera. And Chuck Yeager aspired to soar through the wild blue yonder from his first flight. For Shortcut Sharks, Fountain Ave. is such an inspiration. This sliver of a street ignites a realization that there could be a faster way across Hollywood. Though its virtues and lanes are widely known and traveled, *The Old Shortcutter's Trail* still serves as a valuable alternate to the beastly Sunset Blvd. snag.

THE ROUTE

Westbound starting at Gower St., take Fountain Ave. all the way across Hollywood till it ends at La Cienega Blvd.

BEST HOURS/DIRECTION

With each passing year, the major intersections at La Brea and Highland back up farther and farther at rush hour. For this reason, the *Trail* is best traveled at non-rush hour in either direction.

TIPS

Be sure to stay in the right-hand lane to avoid the dreaded Lefties as you blast through this Hollywood thoroughfare. After 4:00 p.m. the outside lanes are clear between Highland and La Cienega, making passing maneuvers more palatable. For fun, try watching the tow trucks mercilessly haul a batch of BMW's, Volvos, and Jeep Cherokees to the hoosegow.

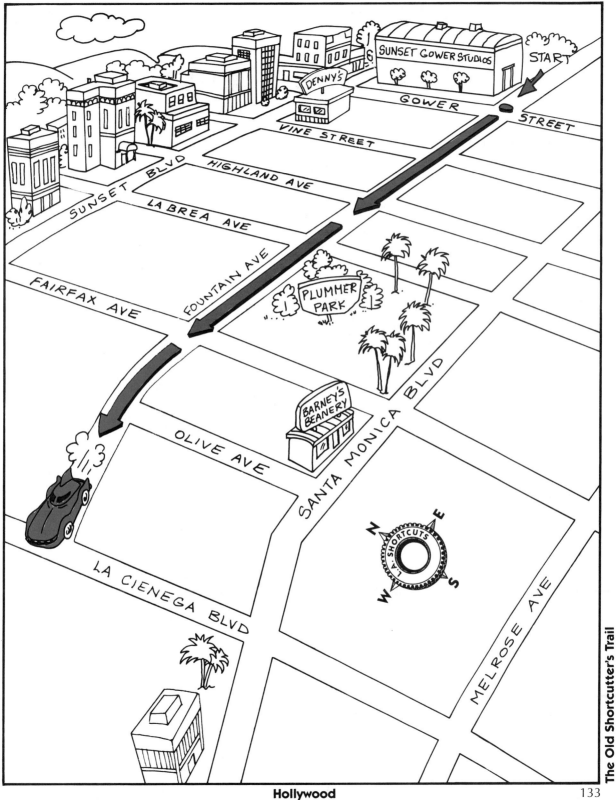

The Old Shortcutter's Trail

On Golden Temple
(Hollywood Freeway to Downtown)

SHORTCUT TIME:
7 minutes

T. GUIDE PAGES:
34, 35, 44

THE SCOOP

The Hollywood Freeway is a great road — between midnight and 4 a.m. The rest of the time it proudly claims fifth place on the list of the world's busiest freeways. The search for salvation from this Plagueway has left many pilgrims spiritually unfulfilled. Until, that is, an apparition in the form of a 45-foot Caltrans cone heralded the entrance to *Golden Temple*. Sanctify yourself on this pious passageway. Who knows...it just could "altar" your driving life.

THE ROUTE

Southbound on the Hollywood Freeway, bail out at Vermont Ave. and follow the off-ramp south to Beverly Blvd. Turn east on Beverly, and when you hit the strange intersection of Virgil, Temple, Beverly, and Silverlake Blvds., go straight on Silverlake. At the underpass, veer right and go up the hill to Temple St. Turn east on Temple and worship your way Downtown.

BEST HOURS/DIRECTION

Temple is open 24 hours a day in either direction.

TIPS

Take this shortcut when your freeway frustrations peak, though the Vermont Ave. exit and then the intersection at Virgil Ave. may test your patience. Still, if your original destination lies beyond Downtown, you can always jump back onto the Hollywood Freeway at Hope St.

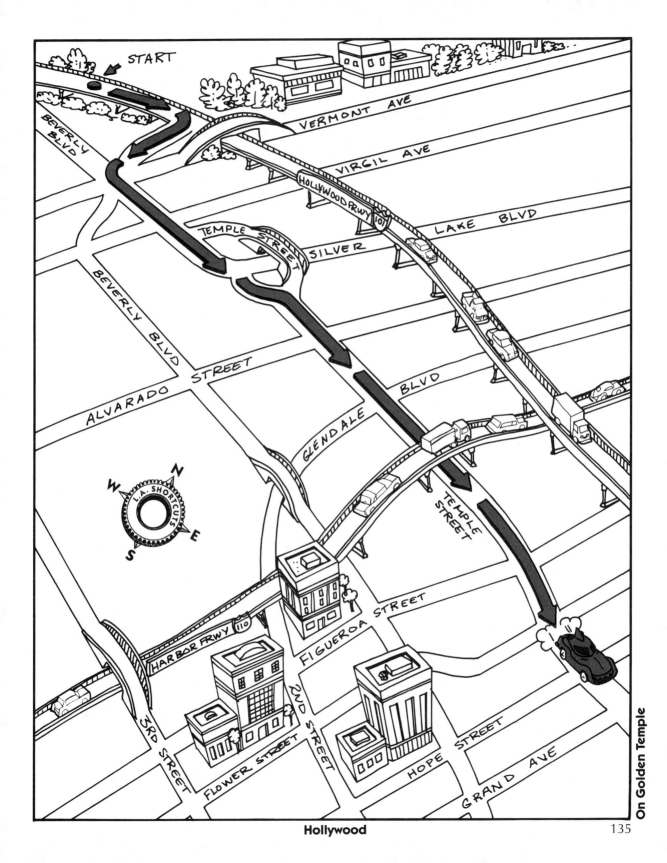

The Road to Casablanca
(Short-Range Hollywood Blvd. Alternate)

<u>**SHORTCUT TIME:**</u>
5 minutes

<u>**T. GUIDE PAGE:**</u>
34

THE SCOOP
This route was born out of a long-standing California tradition: the search for the perfect burrito. But it delivers more than just a hill of refried beans. It slings you behind the enemy lines of weekend warriors on Hollywood Blvd. Anyone familiar with the gawkers and cruisers who bottle up the Boulevard after 6 p.m. will appreciate this godsend. You'll speed behind the scenes of what we call "the miracle mile of Hollywood." (Everyone knows that it's a miracle to make it from Vine St. to La Brea on Hollywood Blvd.) And as if this route wasn't a reward in itself, a decent burrito awaits you at the end of the road at the restaurant Casablanca.

THE ROUTE
Beginning at Vine St. turn west on Selma Ave. and follow it all the way to Highland Ave. Make a right on Highland and immediately cross all lanes and jump into the left hand turn-pocket for Hawthorne Ave. Sneak behind Hollywood Blvd. all the way to La Brea Blvd. and continue north or south to the destination of your choice.

BEST HOURS/DIRECTION
This route is great day and night, except early morning and late afternoon, when Caltrans expands the traffic lanes on Highland. At these times, left turns are impossible.

TIPS
Watch for the drainage dips at Ivar; they're guaranteed to toss your tranny into the next county. Westbound, the left turn onto Hawthorne with heavy opposing traffic requires nerves of steel, so proceed with extreme caution. The same goes for eastbounders turning left onto Selma. For those so inclined, the Hollywood High athletic field on Hawthorne is a great vista point.

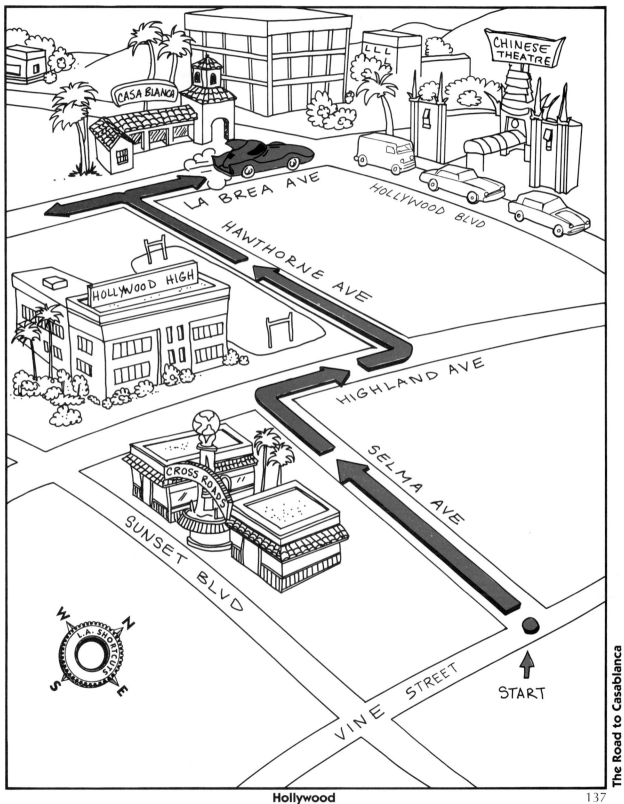

CASA BLANCA

CHINESE THEATRE

LLL

LA BREA AVE

HOLLYWOOD BLVD

HAWTHORNE AVE

HOLLYWOOD HIGH

HIGHLAND AVE

SELMA AVE

CROSS ROADS

SUNSET BLVD

W N S E

L.A. SHORTCUTS

VINE STREET

START

The Road to Casablanca

The Supermarket Sweep
(Santa Monica Blvd./Doheny Dr. Intersection Bypass)

SHORTCUT TIME:
1 minute

T. GUIDE PAGE:
33

THE SCOOP
The Supermarket Sweep is one of the few unspoiled corner-choppers left in this part of town. With two twists of the wheel you'll avoid the dreaded intersection of Santa Monica Blvd. and Doheny Dr. Wave to the unruly hordes of bargain shoppers as you sweep by the side entrance of the Pavilions supermarket parking lot.

THE ROUTE
From Santa Monica Blvd. westbound, turn north on Robertson Blvd. and go one block to Keith Ave. Turn west on Keith passing the supermarket parking lot on your left and follow as it curves right and ends on Doheny Dr.

BEST HOURS/DIRECTION
Naturally, the best bargains can be found during rush hour, but it's discount driving any time in either direction.

TIPS
Small people in big cars are the only obstacles on this corner-cutter. They lunge out of the parking lot like grunion running up the beach to deposit their eggs.

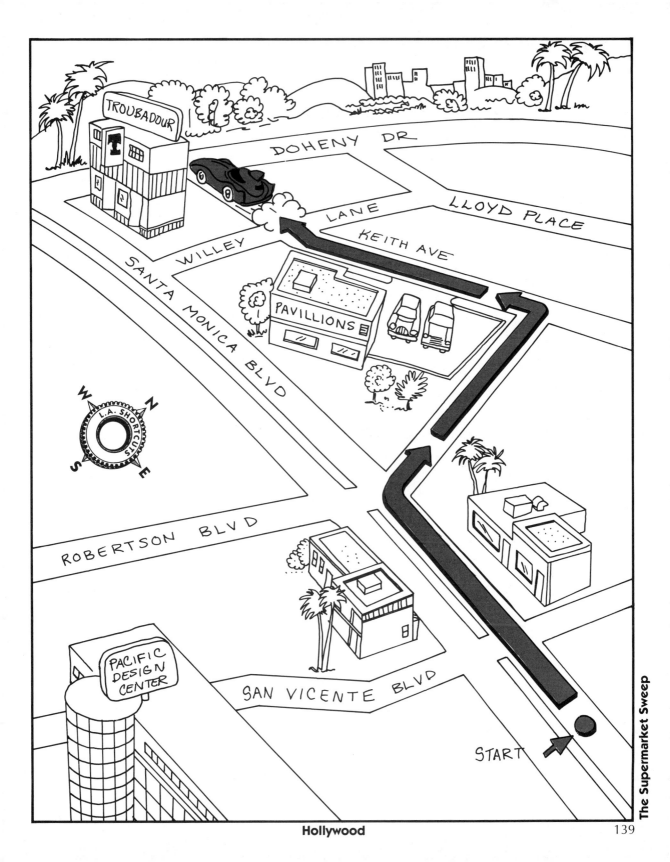

TROUBADOUR

DOHENY DR

LLOYD PLACE

LANE

KEITH AVE

WILLEY

SANTA MONICA BLVD

PAVILLIONS

W N
L.A. SHORTCUTS
S E

ROBERTSON BLVD

PACIFIC DESIGN CENTER

SAN VICENTE BLVD

START

The Supermarket Sweep

Weeping Willoughby
(East/West Hollywood Artery)

SHORTCUT TIME:
8 minutes

T. GUIDE PAGES:
33, 34

THE SCOOP

History is full of great unanswered mysteries: Who shot JFK? Is professional wrestling really a put on? Is Ted Koppel's hair a rug, or what? But there's one puzzling question that stands above the rest: Why the hell does anyone drive on Santa Monica Blvd.? This sad excuse for a major thoroughfare never gives a moment's relief from careening busses and bumper-to-bumper traffic. It's the mecca of Metalheads. That's why we wept for joy when we found a peaceful, residential alternate just two blocks south. Don't forget you're hanky when you whip down *Weeping Willoughby*.

THE ROUTE

Starting at La Cienega Blvd., take Willoughby through all the stop signs to Vine St.

BEST HOURS/DIRECTION

No matter what time of day or day of the week, this route never gets crowded.

TIPS

Students of the "California rolling stop" technique will enjoy this baker's dozen of four-way stop signs along the way. Stay in the right-hand lane when crossing the major streets to avoid the Lefties. Fairfax Ave. is a long light, so you should properly time your approach to try and make the green light. For a good laugh, pull in curbside and check out the sideshow at the La Brea Circus market.

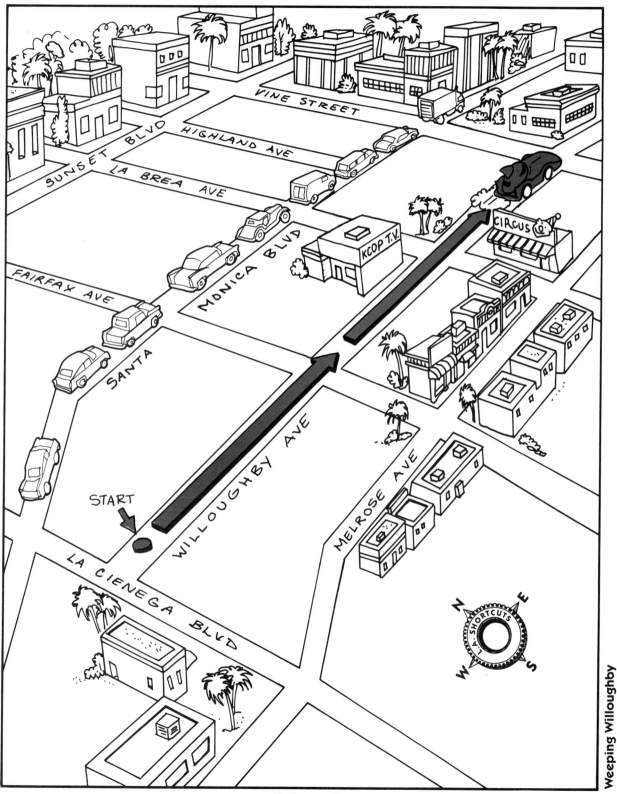

Weeping Willoughby

Wilshire to Melrose in a Snap
(North/South La Cienega Alternate to West Hollywood)

SHORTCUT TIME:
3 minutes

T. GUIDE PAGES:
33, 42

THE SCOOP
Without a doubt, the Miracle Mile is the most aptly named area in the city, for it's a miracle if you can travel a mile. Worse still, driving north from Wilshire during rush hour makes you feel like a mastodon stuck in the prehistoric muck of the La Brea Tar Pits. Don't waste your fossil fuel on La Cienega; come to where the air is Sweetzer.

THE ROUTE
Westbound on Wilshire Blvd. just before San Vicente Blvd., make a quick right and head north on Sweetzer Ave. You'll discover how sweet it is when you arrive at Melrose Ave., far ahead of the lumbering dinosaurs.

BEST HOURS/DIRECTION
The *Snap* gets maximum results during rush hour.

TIPS
Traveling westbound on Wilshire, look for the Big 5 Sporting Goods store, and hang a big right. You'll encounter little flow resistance as you whisk through the outer rim of the Borscht Belt. However, there are occasional mobile obstacles that you must avoid at all costs — babbling blue-haired ladies in late model Buicks.

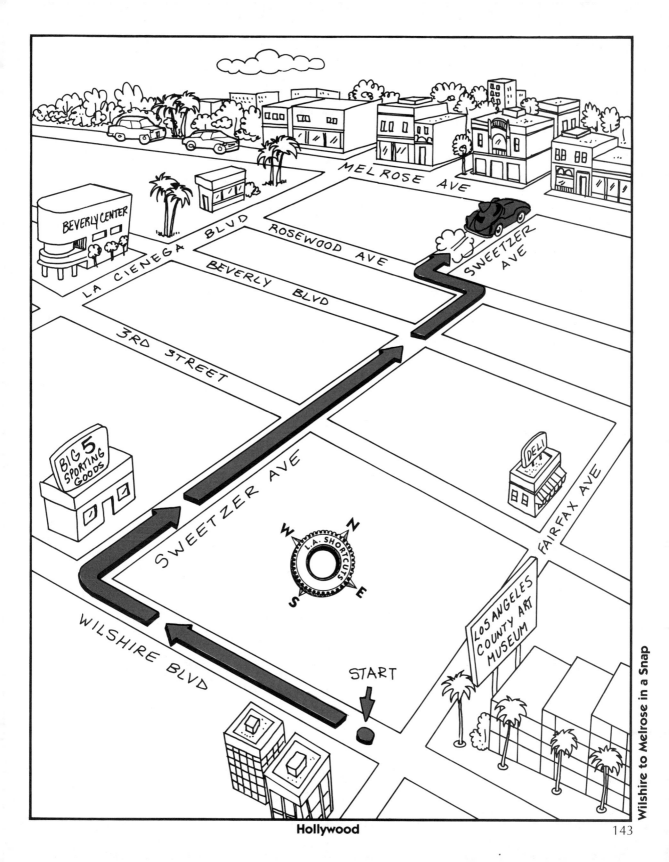

Wilshire to Melrose in a Snap

The Wilton North Report Goes South

(North/South Artery From The Santa Monica Freeway to East Hollywood)

SHORTCUT TIME:
12 minutes

T. GUIDE PAGES:
34, 43

THE SCOOP

Though the title of this shortcut may sound like a trade-paper epitaph for the biggest bomb ever to explode in the face of the Fox Network, *"The Wilton North Report"*, it's actually a well-scripted shortcut. Running through the outer fringes of east Hollywood, this north/south corridor out-performs any show Fox could ever produce. Those of you who once favored the slow-going on Western, Van Ness and Vermont will reap high ratings on this backdoor beat.

THE ROUTE

Eastbound on the Santa Monica Freeway, get off at Crenshaw Blvd. and follow until it ends at Wilshire Blvd. Turn east on Wilshire and proceed to Wilton Pl., where you'll turn north and smoke your tires all the way into East Hollywood.

BEST HOURS/DIRECTION

Wilton cooks during normal business hours, but it's also great for northbound early-fringe and southbound late-fringe travel.

TIPS

Like any great inner-city shortcut, you'll face a surplus of lame-brained Lefties ignoring the "No Left Turn" signs. Between Beverly and 3rd St., beware of the nasty curve where the road quickly narrows. Between Melrose and Santa Monica, traffic occasionally gets backed up. Have patience and you'll soon be zipping past the landmark edifice from which *"The Wilton North Report"* broadcast once dribbled.

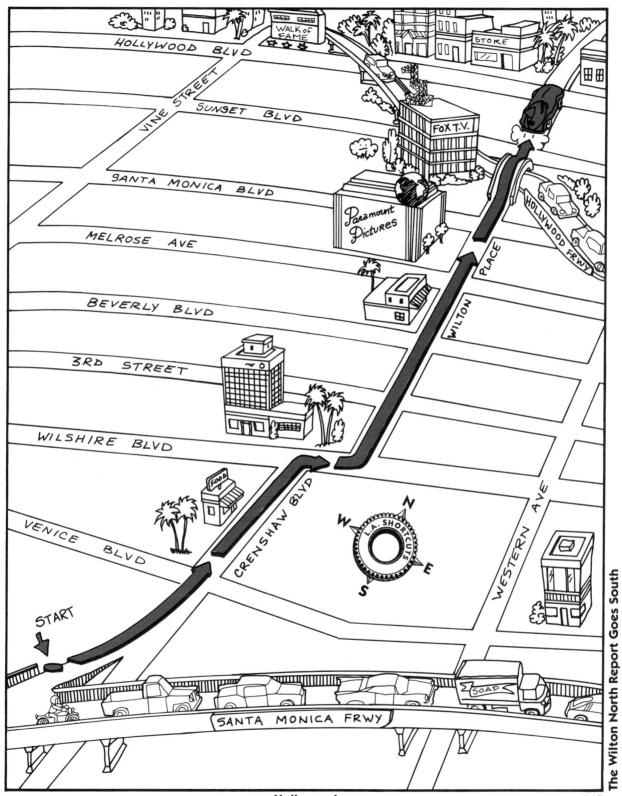

The Wilton North Report Goes South

The Valley

Opportunity. That's exactly what L.A.'s early land barons saw when they looked north upon the arid flatlands below the Santa Monica Mountains. These shrewd businessmen envisioned tract homes, convenience stores, gallerias... the good things in life. They conspired to open the floodgates of water from the Owens Valley, then scooped up land quicker than you can say "What a dweeb!" Rampant development soon transformed this once-pastoral plain into the suburban squalor known in some circles as "The Pit."

Perhaps the best thing we can say about the Valley is that the speculators and developers made it easy to find your way around. After all, who can get lost on boulevards laid out in a north/south and east/west grid? Still, it's of little consolation to know which direction you're headed when you're not making any forward progress.

With plenty of alternate streets to choose from, the challenge of getting there quicker becomes an issue of the quality of your drive over the quantity of the routes. The Valley is the one area left where there's still a vast uncharted frontier of shortcuts. We encourage those with heavy duty air conditioning to venture out and blaze new trails.

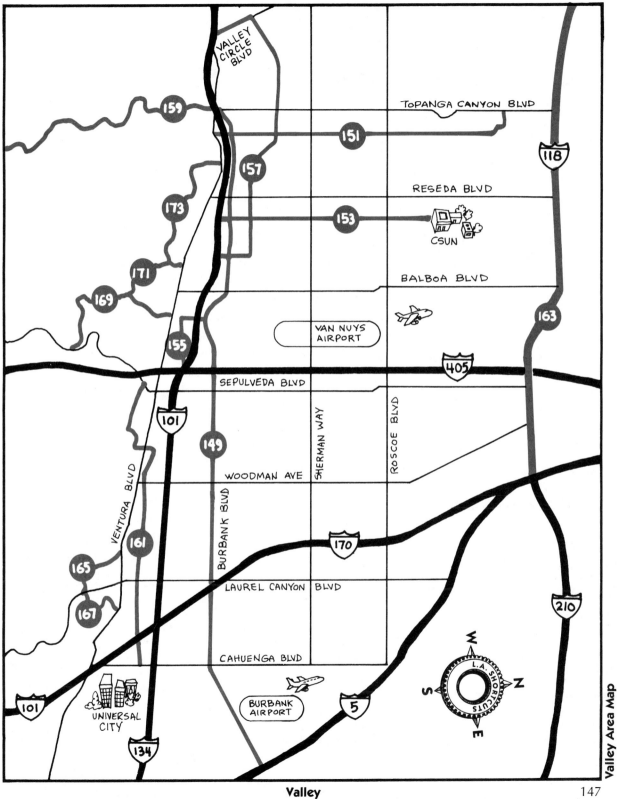

Valley Area Map

The Burbank Blvd. Dash

(East/West Alternate to the Ventura Freeway)

SHORTCUT TIME:
12 minutes

T. GUIDE PAGES:
17, 21, 22, 23, 24

THE SCOOP

When the city planners gathered for their annual San Fernando Valley burger barbecue, engineer Roscoe Saticoy was struck with a brainstorm. Glancing at his meat patty, Saticoy thought what better way to design a street system for the Valley than the grid-like burn marks on his burger? The rest is history. Today if you'd look up the definitions of parallel and perpendicular in the dictionary, you would find a picture of the Valley. Unfortunately, all street grids were not created equal. When The Pack is getting burned on the 101 and Ventura Blvd., you'll savor Burbank Blvd. as a rare morsel for true road gourmets.

THE ROUTE

You can pick up Burbank Blvd. anywhere between the Golden State Freeway (in Burbank) and Reseda Blvd. (in Reseda). Once you're on it, it's Burbank Blvd. all the way.

BEST HOURS/DIRECTION

Burbank Blvd. cooks in both directions all day.

TIPS

Burbank is an all-purpose road; it can be used for long stretches or short hops. This route was timed between the Hollywood and San Diego Plagueways. Compulsive shoppers be warned: You'll find everything from lumber to pianos on this bountiful boulevard. Once in the Sepulveda Dam area, keep that utility eye fixed on those daredevil model airplane owners who occasionally dive-bomb convertibles.

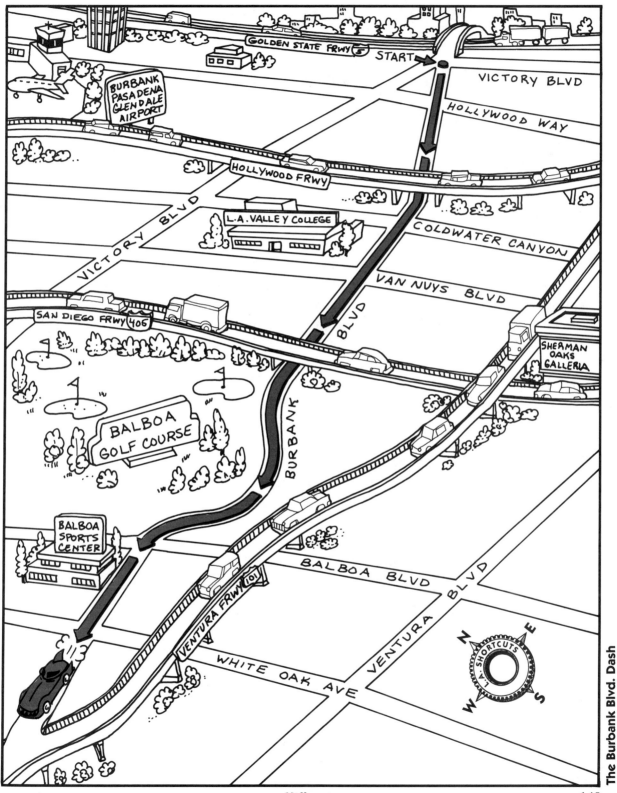

The Burbank Blvd. Dash

Valley

The Canoga Cannon
(North/South Topanga Canyon Bypass in the West Valley)

SHORTCUT TIME:
11 minutes

T. GUIDE PAGES:
6, 12, 13

THE SCOOP

When professionals set out to break land-speed records, they head for the long, flat, and wide expanse of the Bonneville Salt Flats. In this same spirit, Shortcut Sharks abandon the freeways for the long, flat, avenues of the Valley. A record breaker is the fast blast of *The Canoga Cannon*. Streaking you from the used car lots and discount houses near the Ventura Freeway to the railroad tracks and tumbleweeds of Chatsworth, it represents the best of what the Valley has to offer, while avoiding the slow-moving Ambivalenties on Topanga Canyon Blvd.

THE ROUTE

Use Canoga Ave. as an alternate to De Soto Ave. or Topanga Canyon Blvd. going north or south in the Valley.

BEST HOURS/DIRECTION

The Canoga Cannon is heavy artillery at any time in either direction.

TIPS

The *Cannon* hits the city's "top ten" list for its smoothly-timed and far-spaced traffic signals. But before you go full gung-ho, make sure your air conditioning system is fully charged and ready for action. Traveling north from the Ventura Freeway, beware of an urban development nightmare: the Warner Center. It's our hope that one day their next door neighbor, Rockwell International, might inadvertently use it for target practice.

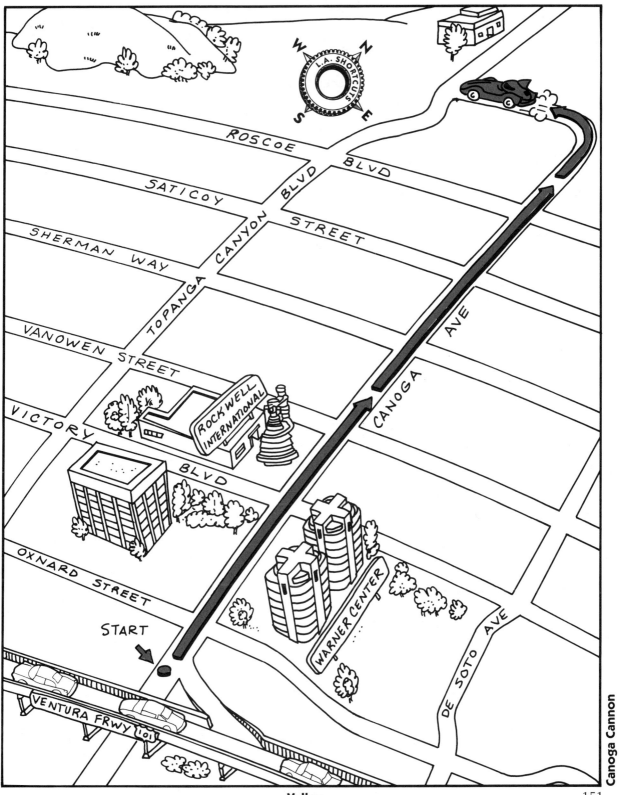

ROSCOE BLVD BLVD

SATICOY BLVD STREET

SHERMAN WAY

TOPANGA CANYON

VANOWEN STREET

CANOGA AVE

VICTORY

ROCKWELL INTERNATIONAL

BLVD

OXNARD STREET

START

WARNER CENTER

DE SOTO AVE

VENTURA FRWY 101

L.A. SHORTCUTS

Canoga Cannon

El Rayo X

(North/South Artery in the West Valley)

SHORTCUT TIME:
8 minutes

T. GUIDE PAGES:
7, 14, 21

THE SCOOP
Student pilots are taught to always keep a landmark in sight for navigational purposes. Well, have you ever been stuck in the middle of the Valley on a hot, smoggy day with no visibility — where every corner looks alike? It's a feeling that would even panic pilots with the most righteous stuff. Well, fear no more. *El Rayo X* is a navigator's guiding light, slicing a supersonic north/south course through the core of this inferno.

THE ROUTE
Beginning at Ventura Blvd. between Reseda Blvd. and White Oak Ave., hop on Lindley Ave. north and let the Pack eat your vapor trail as you streak up to Nordhoff St.

BEST HOURS/DIRECTION
You're cleared for takeoff on *El Rayo X* 24 hours a day in either direction.

TIPS
The traffic signals on Lindley Ave. are so well-timed that to hit a red light would just about classify as a miracle. It's a straight-arrow run to the entrance of CSUN where "tube steak" aficionados will be blessed with a bonus — Cupid Dog (hot dogs from heaven) at Nordhoff.

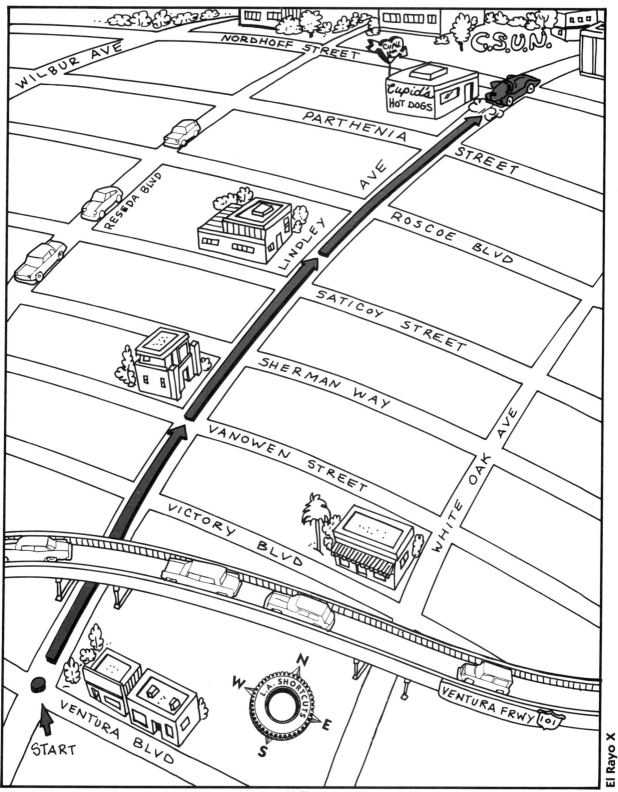

El Rayo X

Hayvenhurst Can't Wait

(Back Door Entry onto the Ventura Freeway)

THE SCOOP

Diehard Shortcut Sharks will do anything to avoid the vile Ventura Freeway on-slaught. And where there's a will, there's a way around. This route won't take you very far, but it bypasses the masses by discreetly infiltrating the last Ventura Freeway eastbound on-ramp before the 405 cloverleaf.

THE ROUTE

Eastbound on Burbank Blvd., go south on Louise Ave. Cross the Ventura Freeway and make the first left on Killion St. Follow Killion as it curves south and turns into Amestoy Ave. Follow Amestoy for about a half-mile, and then turn left on Magnolia Ave. Go east to the Ventura Freeway on-ramp.

BEST HOURS/DIRECTION

This is a one-way route going eastbound. You'll get the best results whenever the Ventura Freeway is clogged.

TIPS

In deference to the environment, someone saw fit to leave a mighty oak tree in the middle of Magnolia Ave. We recommend that you try to avoid it. The light at Balboa can be annoying, so rock-and-roll your car to trip the signal sensors and get that green light.

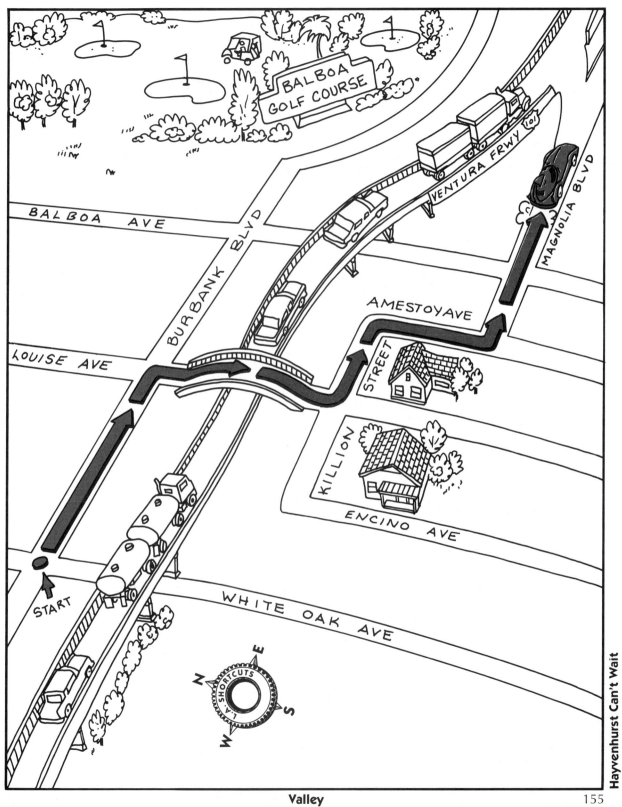

BALBOA GOLF COURSE

BALBOA AVE

BURBANK BLVD

VENTURA FRWY

MAGNOLIA BLVD

AMESTOY AVE

LOUISE AVE

STREET

KILLION

ENCINO AVE

START

WHITE OAK AVE

N E S W

L.A. SHORTCUTS

Hayvenhurst Can't Wait

Kick in the Oxnard

(East/West Mid-Valley Alternate to the Ventura Freeway)

SHORTCUT TIME:
19 minutes

T. GUIDE PAGES:
5, 12, 14, 21, 100

THE SCOOP

For those who depend upon the Ventura Plagueway for their daily commute we pose this simple question: Is it worth enduring three years of teeth-gnashing agony for the construction of one measly extra lane? The truth is, it doesn't matter how you feel about this issue because you're bound to suffer the consequences — unless you pick up the *Kick* for the ride of your life. It'll whip you past the deadly 101 crawl.

THE ROUTE

Westbound on the Ventura Freeway, get off at White Oak Ave. and go north to Oxnard St. Turn west on Oxnard and follow the railroad tracks until Oxnard turns into Topham St. near Cahill St. Follow Topham as it angles to the right and ends at Victory Blvd. Jog to the left on Victory and continue west for the long stretch (6 miles) to Valley Circle. Go south on Valley Circle to the Ventura Freeway westbound or just hang it up in Calabasas.

BEST HOURS/DIRECTION

We prescribe a dose of this freeway remedy only during times of heavy congestion or construction on the 101, but it's also great any time of day.

TIPS

Though this fast-paced route runs nearly 10 miles from end to end, it's unlikely you'll need to use it all the way. But to get around long trouble spots on the 101, you can't do better. And if you've ever wondered where glorious Ventura Blvd. ends, *Kick in the Oxnard* takes you right by its pitiful conclusion. No boutiques here...just a mound of dirt and a curb.

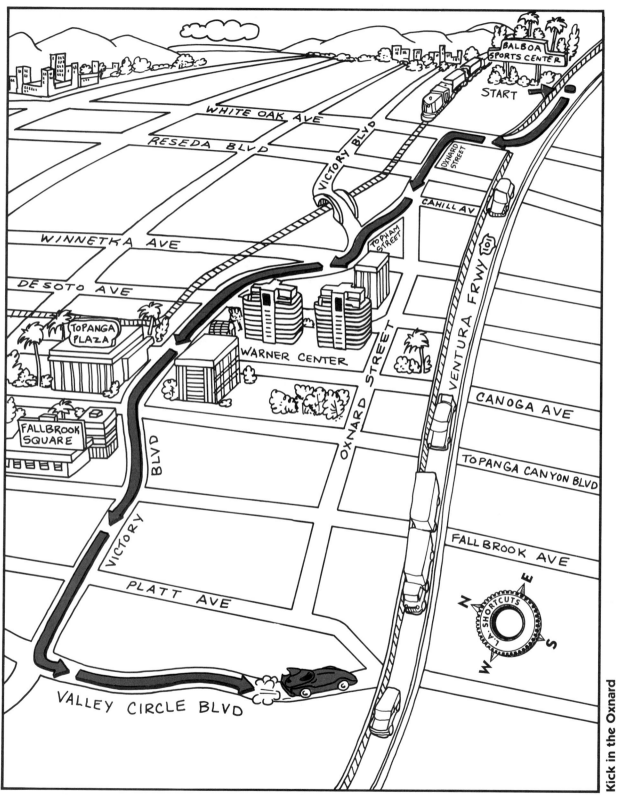

Kick in the Oxnard

Life's a Beach

(From the West Valley to the Beach)

SHORTCUT TIME:
15 minutes

T. GUIDE PAGES:
13, 109, 115

THE SCOOP

Evolutionary theory has it that when Southern California man first crawled out of the ocean he was sporting Jimmy Z's jams and wrap-around shades. A few million years later, this particular species now thrives throughout the Valley. On any blistering hot day, this genus answers to its primordial biological urge to migrate back to the sea. Lemming-like hordes flood every conceivable avenue to the waves with suicidal zeal. Just one route guarantees survival of the fittest: *Life's a Beach*. Older than a fossilized dinosaur turd, this route has proved its reliability throughout the ages.

THE ROUTE

Get off the Ventura Freeway at Topanga Canyon Blvd. and head south all the way through the canyon to the beach.

BEST HOURS/DIRECTION

Great any time except weekday rush hours, both morning and evening.

TIPS

Topanga is a very winding road, so keep it slow and in control. This well- traveled road is home to the Shortcut Shark's natural predator: The CHP. You'll find them lurking on most straightaways, so keep a wary eye. Once inside the village of To- panga, avoid the People That Time Forgot... spaced-out "shroom-gobblers" search- ing for Joni Mitchell at the old Mermaid Cafe.

START

VENTURA FRWY 101

TOPANGA CANYON BLVD

TOPANGA

OLD TOPANGA CANYON RD

MARKET

N
W E
S
L.A. SHORTCUTS

TOPANGA CANYON BLVD

PACIFIC COAST HIGHWAY

GAS

FOOD

Life's A Beach

The Moorpark Motorway
(East/West Alternate to the Ventura Freeway)

SHORTCUT TIME:
14 minutes

T. GUIDE PAGES:
22, 23

THE SCOOP

You can count on just three things in life: death, taxes, and heavy congestion on the Ventura Freeway. It's the world's busiest road, clocking in at 267,000 vehicles per day. That's 11,125 cars per hour! It's no surprise that the stretch between the Hollywood and San Diego Plagueways often looks like a Pic 'n' Save parking lot during the Christmas holidays. Why sit and steam in your own juices at your favorite on-ramp? Take our heavenly alternative, the Moorpark Motorway. It's a little known fact that God didn't rest on the seventh day; He created Moorpark.

THE ROUTE

Starting at Cahuenga Blvd., turn west on Moorpark St. and whip straight to Van Nuys Blvd. Turn south on Van Nuys, cross Ventura Blvd, and immediately bail out with a turn west onto Dickens St. Make a quick turn south on Cedros Ave. and then turn west on Greenleaf Ave. Follow Greenleaf to Sepulveda Blvd. (If you need to get over the pass, refer to *How the Other Half Lives*.)

BEST HOURS/DIRECTION

There are two ways to use this route. First, take it any time you spot heavy traffic on the Ventura Freeway. Second, you can use it as an escape valve if you're already on the freeway and nothing's moving.

TIPS

Unlike most of L.A.'s streets, the traffic lights on Moorpark are well timed if you keep a steady pace. Watch out for hidden dips between Coldwater and Van Nuys, as they'll sneak up on you. At Radford Ave. watch for natives washing their designer jeans on the banks of the picturesque Tujunga Wash.

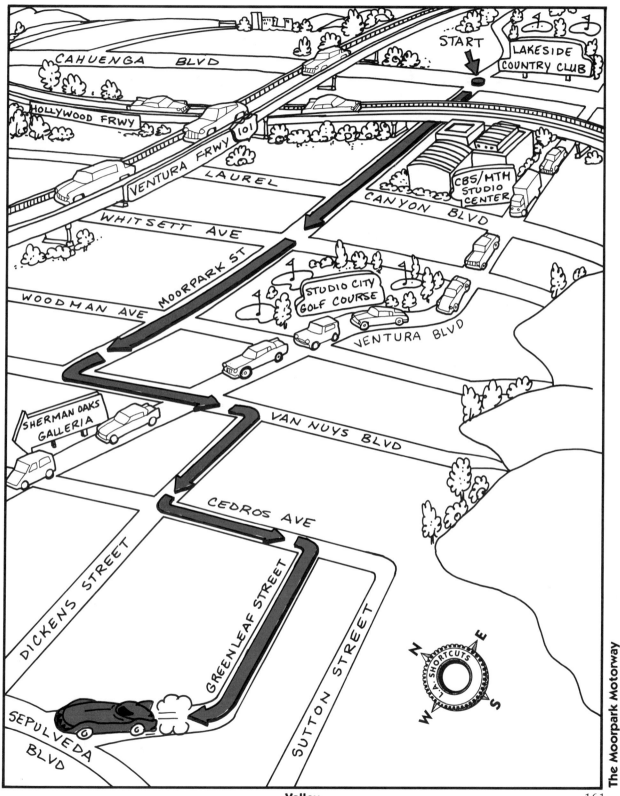

The Moorpark Motorway

Not Just Any Freeway
(East/West Artery in the North Valley)

SHORTCUT TIME:
12 minutes

T. GUIDE PAGES:
4, 6, 7, 8

THE SCOOP

At one time, L.A.'s freeway system resembled the cardio-vascular system of a young stud. Now entering middle age, its arteries are clogged and suffering from the daily grind of dangerously high blood pressure. Massive congestive heart failure could strike at any moment. Though one aorta does not a healthy heart make, the 118 Freeway still pumps with the vigor of a young buck.

THE ROUTE

Pick up the 118 Freeway anywhere between the 210 Freeway and Simi Valley and get ready to sail in either direction, east or west. Note: The official name of this freeway is the Simi Valley - San Fernando Valley Freeway, but we minimalist humans refer to it simply as "the 118."

BEST HOURS/DIRECTION

Though the 118 suffers the usual congestion at rush hour, it's still faster than any side street.

TIPS

One disadvantage to this route is that you've just about have to live out here to use it. But look on the bright side; if you lived here you'd be home by now.

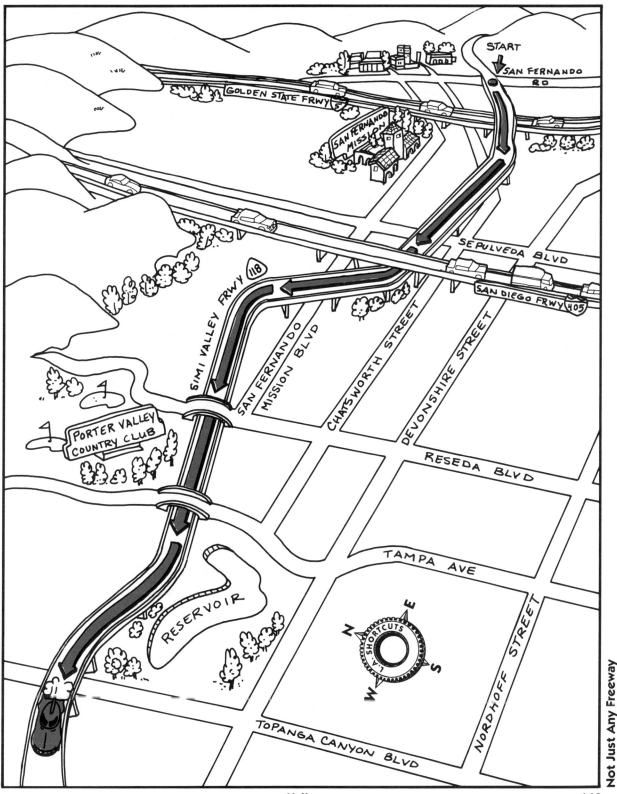

START
↓ SAN FERNANDO RD

GOLDEN STATE FRWY 5

SAN FERNANDO MISSION

SEPULVEDA BLVD

SAN DIEGO FRWY 405

SIMI VALLEY FRWY 118

SAN FERNANDO MISSION BLVD

CHATSWORTH STREET

DEVONSHIRE STREET

PORTER VALLEY COUNTRY CLUB

RESEDA BLVD

TAMPA AVE

RESERVOIR

L.A. SHORTCUTS

N E S W

NORDHOFF STREET

TOPANGA CANYON BLVD

Not Just Any Freeway

Out on the Terrace
(Short-Range Laurel Canyon/Ventura Blvd. Bypass)

SHORTCUT TIME:
2 minutes

T. GUIDE PAGE:
23

THE SCOOP

Driving this short-but-sweet shortcut is like making the big leap from training wheels to a two wheeler. Once you learn it, there's no turning back. It circumvents one of the worst intersections in the Valley (Laurel and Ventura) by taking you on a pleasant suburban jog. Wave good-bye forever to the rubber-necking boutique junkies who paralyze the area. No more waiting for that endless stream of traffic to clear for the left turn onto Ventura Blvd. Just like the thrill of balancing on two wheels, this route will give you a kick for its ease in outsmarting The Pack.

THE ROUTE

Northbound on Laurel Canyon Blvd. just before Ventura Blvd., turn west on Laurel Terrace Dr. Follow Laurel Terrace until it ends at Ventura, or continue north on Whitsett Ave.

BEST HOURS/DIRECTION

This route is great any time in either direction.

TIPS

When going north on Laurel Canyon, be careful making the left turn onto Laurel Terrace. There is no signal to protect you from oncoming traffic. The neighborhood may seem sedated, but it's full of speed traps. So, though you'll be tempted to crank through the area — don't!

LAUREL CANYON BLVD

START

STORE

TIRES

THRIFTY DRUG

LAUREL TERRACE DR

VENTURA BLVD

FAST PHOTO

STUDIO CITY GOLF COURSE

WHITSETT AVE

L.A. SHORTCUTS

N E S W

Out on A Terrace

Ray of Sunshine

(Short-Range Laurel Canyon/Ventura Blvd. Bypass)

<table>
<tr><td>SHORTCUT TIME:</td><td>T. GUIDE PAGE:</td></tr>
<tr><td>1 minute</td><td>23</td></tr>
</table>

THE SCOOP

For those who've found refuge on *Out on a Terrace* you now have *Ray of Sunshine* to guide you eastward around the Laurel Canyon/Ventura Blvd. bottleneck bash. Your stormy struggle will finally clear as you break through the clouds to Ventura Blvd.

THE ROUTE

Northbound on Laurel Canyon Blvd., just before Ventura Blvd., turn east onto Sunshine Terrace, go one block and turn north on Carpenter Ave. Take Carpenter to Ventura and drill your way through the masses.

BEST HOURS/DIRECTION

This route is great any day in either direction.

TIPS

Resist the temptation to crank through these residential streets, because there's a well-hidden grammar school on Carpenter. If the crossing guard doesn't get you, an angry officer might. Besides, what's the rush? You're still light years ahead of The Pack.

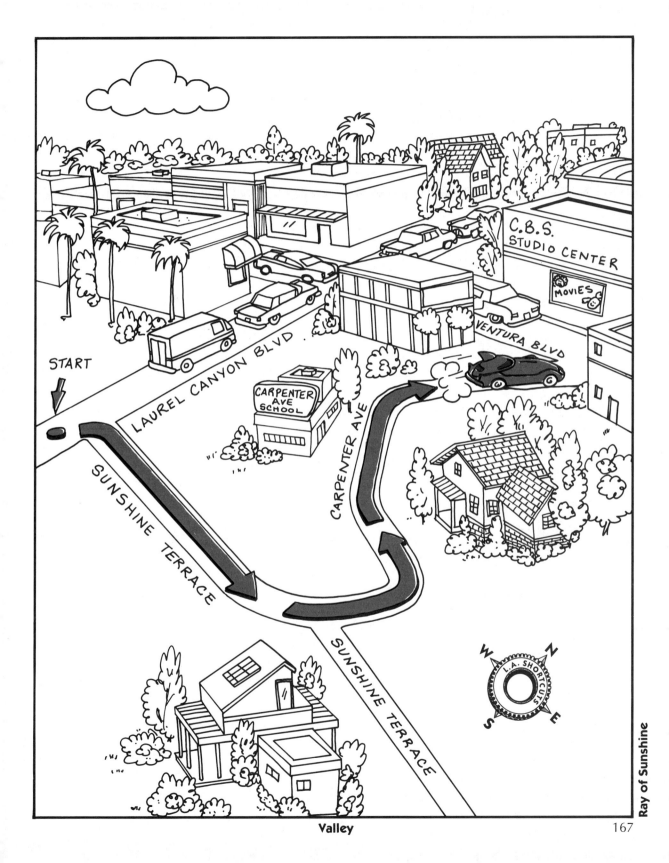

START

LAUREL CANYON BLVD.

CARPENTER AVE SCHOOL

CARPENTER AVE

VENTURA BLVD

C.B.S. STUDIO CENTER

MOVIES

SUNSHINE TERRACE

SUNSHINE TERRACE

W N S E
L.A. SHORTCUTS

Ray of Sunshine

The Valley Dive
(San Diego and Ventura Freeways Interchange Bypass)

SHORTCUT TIME:
7 minutes

T. GUIDE PAGES:
21, 22

THE SCOOP

It may be known as the Sepulveda Pass, but we like to think of it as the Sepulveda Impasse. Though Caltrans won't admit it, we discovered that the 405 freeway is not constructed of concrete, but rather a mixture of flypaper and bubble gum. This explains the notorious daily traffic pileups. It's L.A.'s equivalent of a giant Roach Motel in which cars check in, but never check out. In its place, Valley-goers will want to check out The Valley Dive. It exterminates the wasp's nest at the 405 and Ventura interchange and will parachute you safely to all points north and west.

THE ROUTE

Northbound on the San Diego Freeway in the Sepulveda Pass, exit at Mulholland Dr. Cross back over the freeway and head west on Mulholland Dr. until you get to Calneva Dr. Take the plunge down Calneva about a half-mile to Hayvenhurst Ave. Your ears will pop when you turn north on Hayvenhurst and land in the Valley.

BEST HOURS/DIRECTION

Though this shortcut is great any time in either direction, going south up the hill can be treacherous for four-cylinder econoboxes.

TIPS

Take in the Valley panorama from Mulholland if it's clear enough to see anything. The drop down Calneva will accelerate you to supersonic speeds in a flash, so keep it slow and watch out for residents backing out of their driveways. When Michael Jackson and Bubbles are in town, beware of the autograph hounds lurking outside his compound south of Libbit on Hayvenhurst.

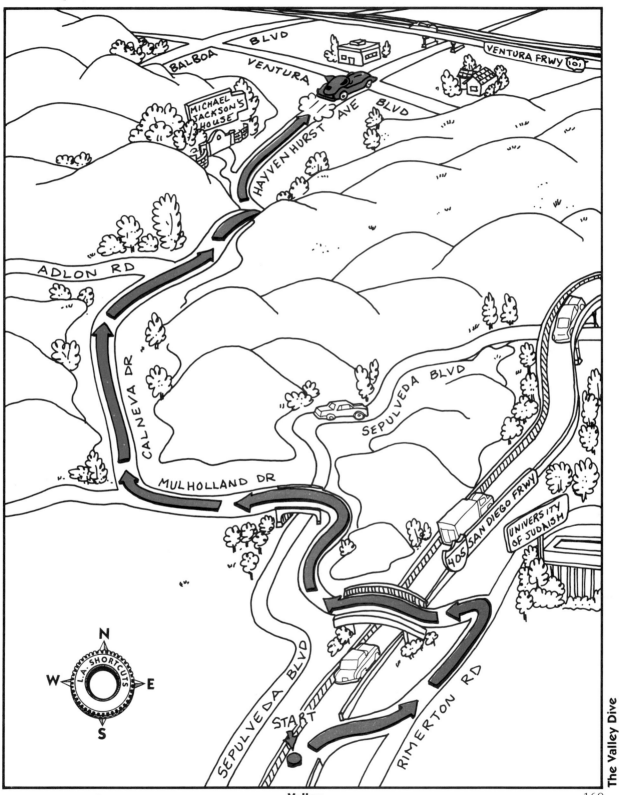

BALBOA BLVD

VENTURA BLVD

VENTURA FRWY 101

MICHAEL JACKSON'S HOUSE

HAYVENHURST AVE BLVD

ADLON RD

CAL NEVA DR

SEPULVEDA BLVD

MULHOLLAND DR

SAN DIEGO FRWY

405

UNIVERSITY OF JUDAISM

N
W E
S
L.A. SHORTCUTS

SEPULVEDA BLVD

START

RIMERTON RD

Valley

The Valley Dive

169

Valley Dive - Part 2
(East/West Ventura Blvd. Alternate)

SHORTCUT TIME: T. GUIDE PAGE:
3 minutes   21

THE SCOOP
Hollywood has taught us that every box office hit is quickly followed by a sequel. And so it goes with shortcuts. This continuation of *The Valley Dive* will keep you off both Venturas — Freeway and Boulevard. It winds through one of the Valley's more "charming" residential areas and rewards you with peace of mind at a shortcut pace.

THE ROUTE
Northbound on Hayvenhurst Ave., turn west on Adlon Rd. and proceed two blocks to Empress Ave. Turn north on Empress, then make a quick turn west onto Mooncrest Dr. Turn north on Nance St., then go a short distance to where it ends at Louise Ave. Turn north on Louise.

BEST HOURS/DIRECTION
Unlike the first *Valley Dive*, there are no steep inclines to slow down this shortcut. It's great 24 hours a day in either direction.

TIPS
Just after turning west onto Adlon, veer to the left where it intersects with Bagio Dr. There's no street sign for Nance St., so look for the dead-end sign on Mooncrest and turn right. You'll now be on Nance.

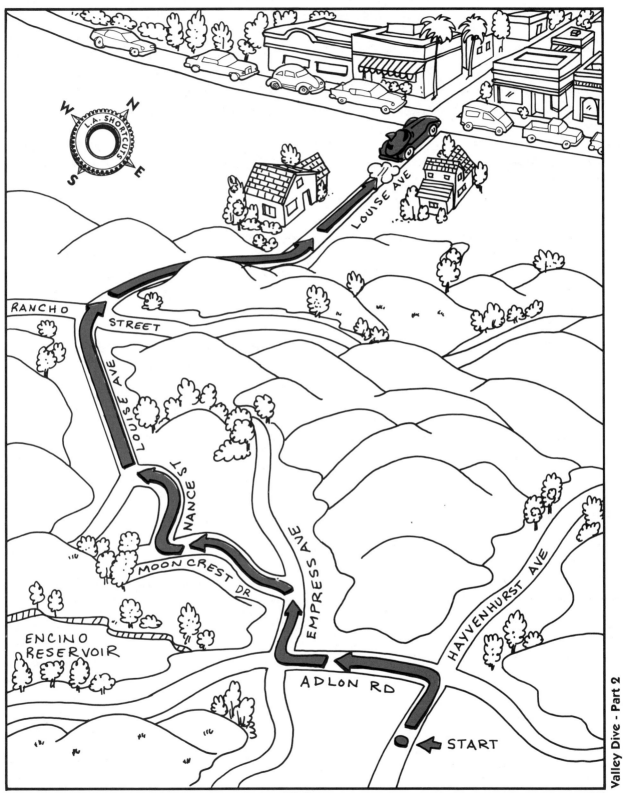

Valley Dive - The Revenge
(East/West Ventura Blvd. Alternate)

SHORTCUT TIME:
7 minutes

T. GUIDE PAGE:
21

THE SCOOP
One successful sequel deserves another, right? Of course! This shortcut was discovered by chasing a strange vehicular parade (a Jag, Range Rover, and Ninja) into the bowels of the mysterious hills of Encino. This relaxing ride meanders through oak-lined lanes graced with ultra-expensive estates. Prepare yourself for culture shock when you reach the intersection of Vanalden and Ventura.

THE ROUTE
Northbound on Louise Ave. before Ventura Blvd., turn west on Rancho St. and follow it past the point where it turns into Valley Vista Blvd. Take Valley Vista until it ends at Nestle Ave. Turn north on Nestle, then turn west on Tarzana St., then bear north onto Avenida Hacienda. Turn west on Wells Dr., and follow it until it ends at Vanalden Ave. Turn north on Vanalden. Presto! You're about 20 blocks ahead of the Metalheads on Ventura Blvd.

BEST HOURS/DIRECTION
Use this route any time you want to circumvent the Slomofos on Ventura Blvd.

TIPS
As with all routes in the *Valley Dive* series, watch for small herds of local hotheads tromping through the area. On Rancho the streets are very tight, but don't let threading the needle distract you from the great entertainment provided by some of the world's most hideous residential wrought iron formations.

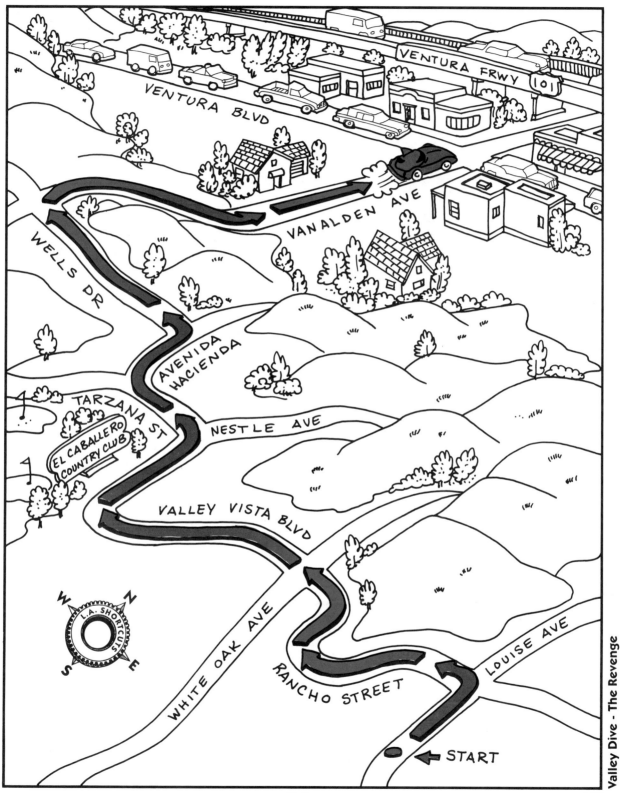

Valley Dive - The Revenge

The Westside and Beaches

When Horace Greeley tried to rid himself of an unruly young scribe by uttering, "Go west, young man!", he never envisioned that millions of malcontents would take him literally. When Greeley's hordes eventually ran out of trails to blaze and faced the Pacific Ocean, they had two choices: build boats and sail on to Hawaii, or open sushi bars and settle the Westside.

Uncomfortable with large bodies of water, they chose the latter and prospered. Ocean breezes and plenty of wide-open spaces enticed them to invite all of their friends and relatives to join them. Unfortunately, they're still coming.

And that's the trouble.

Once hailed as the "Promised Land," the steady influx of new arrivals left no land to be promised. Overdeveloped and densely populated, the Westside and beach areas suffer from irresponsibly unchecked growth. Wide-open boulevards that once provided a Sunday drive every day of the week are now crammed with surly road hogs clawing their way across town. It's no surprise that the Westside has seven of the ten most heavily traveled intersections in all of Los Angeles.

Still, relief does exist. The shortcuts in this chapter will ease you through those Westside bottlenecks faster than a sushi knife slicing through a California roll.

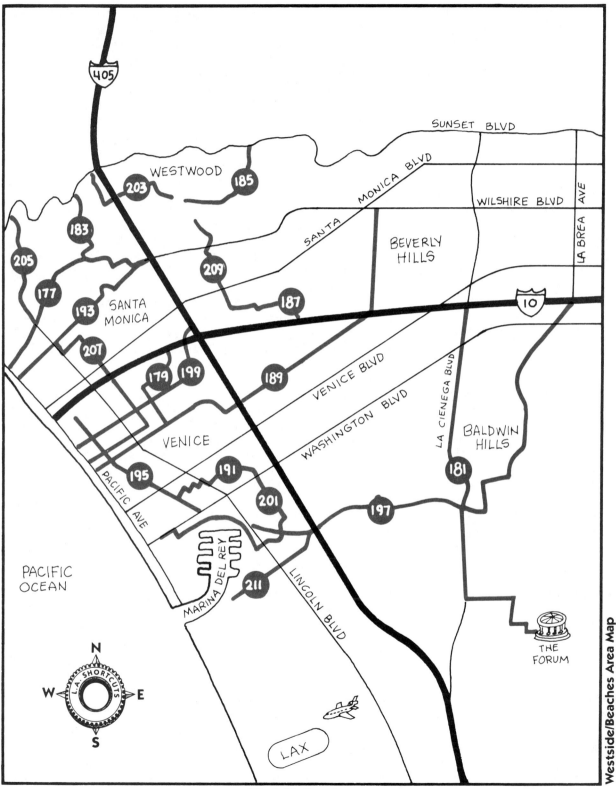

Westside/Beaches Area Map

Beach Blanket Bingo
(Wilshire Blvd. Bypass to the Beach)

SHORTCUT TIME:
9 minutes

T. GUIDE PAGES:
40, 41

THE SCOOP

It's a balmy Saturday afternoon. You and that big, nasty redhead opt for a romantic sunset picnic on the cliffs high above the blue Pacific. But as the sun edges closer to the horizon, you're still barely edging down Wilshire Blvd. Before your chances for romance fade with the setting sun, take San Vicente Blvd. — that vast, green stretch of baby's-butt smooth highway. Crossing 26th St. you enter that fuzzy area where the temperature drops 10 degrees. (Locals call it "the Grey Curtain.") By 7th St. it's foggy and frigid, so you scrap the picnic and head for that hot, nouvelle Jamaican joint on Melrose.

THE ROUTE

Starting at Wilshire Blvd. westbound, get into the right-hand lane when you pass the Veterans Administration Hospital. At San Vicente Blvd. go north and follow as it curves west towards the beach. Crank up *"I Love L.A."* and pound the pedal to the metal all the way to Ocean Blvd.

BEST HOURS/DIRECTION

San Vicente is smooth sailing in either direction any time of day.

TIPS

Antsy Chows dashing to Chin Chin near Barrington occasionally cause a bottleneck, but it won't last long enough to be a problem. Watch out for thrill-seeking joggers on the center greenbelt divider and cyclists who dart in and out of traffic for a quick adrenaline fix.

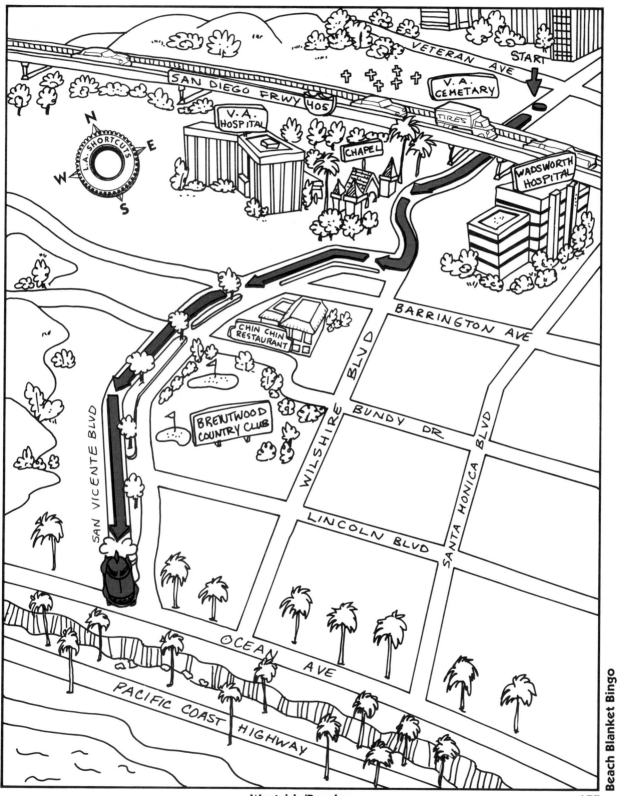

Beach Blanket Bingo

Brock's Beachcomber Trail

(From the Santa Monica Freeway to Venice)

SHORTCUT TIME:
7 minutes

T. GUIDE PAGES:
41, 49

THE SCOOP

It's a picture-postcard day: 92 degrees with unhealthful air quality predicted for the L.A. basin. Feigning your famous deathbed cough, you call in sick and head for the beach. Zipping onto the Santa Monica freeway, wind in your face, cooler by your side, you snicker with glee at your successful deception. At Lincoln Blvd. your snicker turns into a scowl as you discover that half the city is attempting the same ingenious ruse. While you're stuck with the 20-minute grovel to the beach, the few enlightened truants who took *Brock's Beachcomber Trail* are already applying their second coat of coco-aloe-papaya lotion and power lounging on the sand.

THE ROUTE

From the Santa Monica Freeway westbound, get off at Cloverfield Blvd. and turn south. Follow to Ocean Park Blvd. and turn west for one block, then turn south on 23rd St. Follow 23rd until it turns into Walgrove Ave. and proceed to Rose Ave. Turn west on Rose and punch it all the way to the beach.

BEST HOURS/DIRECTION

Forget this route when you're beach-bound late on weekday afternoons. Otherwise it's clear sailing.

TIPS

Southbound on 23rd near the Santa Monica Airport, beware of police speed traps. Rather than forking out $5.00 at the beach parking lot, we suggest looking for a parking spot on Main St.— but make sure you have a fistful of quarters for the hungry parking meters.

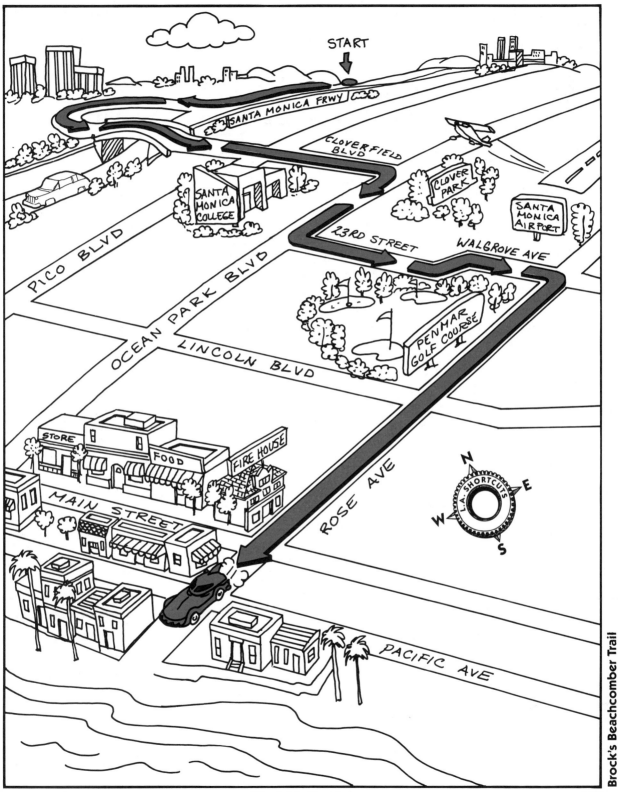

START

SANTA MONICA FRWY

CLOVERFIELD BLVD

CLOVER PARK

SANTA MONICA AIRPORT

SANTA MONICA COLLEGE

PICO BLVD

23RD STREET

WALGROVE AVE

OCEAN PARK BLVD

LINCOLN BLVD

PENMAR GOLF COURSE

STORE

FOOD

FIRE HOUSE

MAIN STREET

ROSE AVE

N
E
W
S
L.A. SHORTCUTS

PACIFIC AVE

Burkow's Fast Break to the Forum

(Crowd Detour into the Forum)

SHORTCUT TIME:
8 minutes

T. GUIDE PAGES:
50, 56, 57

THE SCOOP
A not so funny thing happens on the way to the not so Fabulous Forum: total traffic gridlock. Fans often spend more game time listening to Chick Hearn from their bucket seats than they do from their courtside seats. Our shortcut is a fast break that shoots through the backcourt. This first-round draft pick is a tipoff that's really "magic."

THE ROUTE
Southbound on La Cienega Blvd. just before the entrance to the San Diego Freeway, turn east on Industrial Ave. Go one block and turn south on Hyde Park Blvd. Take Hyde Park to Florence Ave. and turn east. Make the second right turn onto Regent St. Follow Regent to La Brea Ave. and turn south. Just past Manchester Blvd. make a left turn on Nutwood St. and jog to the right while staying on Nutwood. Rejoin the throngs of fans flooding the Forum at Prairie.

BEST HOURS/DIRECTION
It doesn't matter how the Lakers are doing, traffic in and out of the Forum is always chaotic. Our fast break is flawless during any event.

TIPS
Turning east onto Industrial can be a "Hail Mary" for rookies. It looks as though you'll be sucked onto the freeway when suddenly a left turn pocket appears over the crest of the hill. It's a dangerous turn across speeding traffic. The only other obstacle is the strange intersection of Hillcrest and Nutwood. Ignore the arrows and bear to the right.

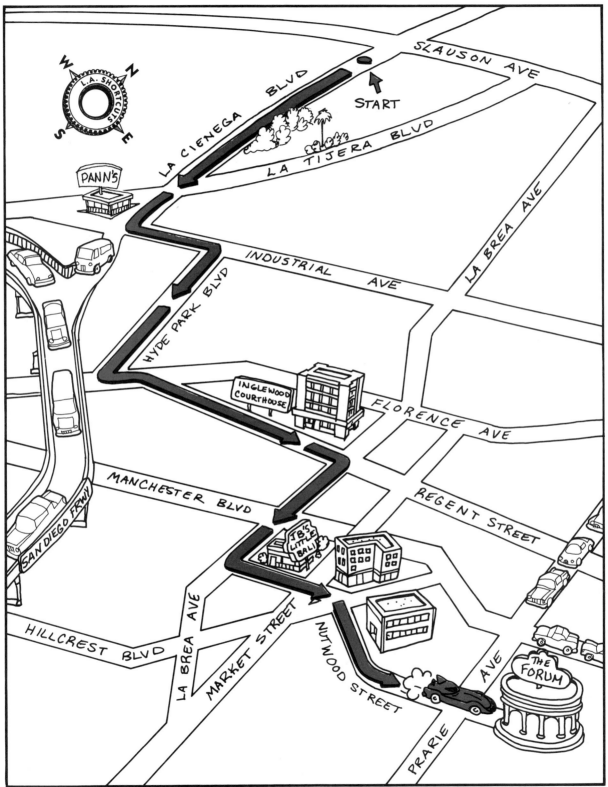

Burkow's Fast Break to the Forum

B.Z.'s Jump
(Barrington Ave. Bypass)

SHORTCUT TIME:
1 minute

T. GUIDE PAGE:
41

THE SCOOP

Brentwood Village was once a tranquil little hamlet nestled among the sprawling mountain estates of the Westside. In the old days, if you happened to stumble upon it you would have found two drug stores and a deli. Now it's teeming above maximum capacity with bored Brentwood housewives and famished flotsam and jetsam looking for good cannelloni. The moral of this tragic tale is to steer clear of Barrington between San Vicente and Sunset Blvd. If you want to ferry between the San Diego Freeway and Brentwood, take a hop down *B.Z.'s Jump*!

THE ROUTE

Going westbound on San Vicente, make a quick right on Montana Ave. and before you finish the turn, make an even quicker left onto Westgate Ave. Continue north on Westgate until it ends at Sunset Blvd.

BEST HOURS/DIRECTION

The *Jump* is great any time in either direction.

TIPS

When turning south onto Westgate from Sunset, make sure your turn signals work! Otherwise you'll quickly become a sardine sandwich. Also, be sure to exercise extreme caution when turning north onto Westgate from Montana — this area is teeming above capacity with Rabidashers, Antsy Chows and Metalheads.

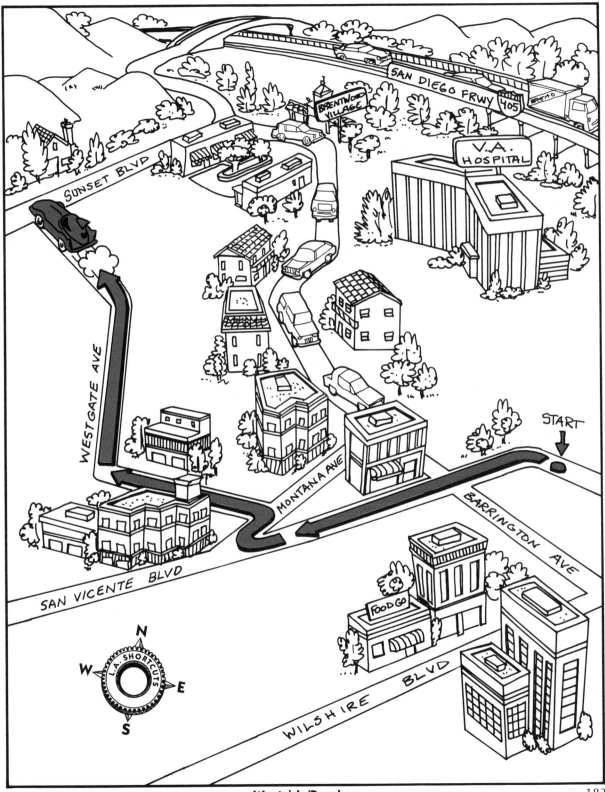

SAN DIEGO FRWY 405

BRENTWOOD VILLAGE

V.A. HOSPITAL

SUNSET BLVD

WESTGATE AVE

START

MONTANA AVE

BARRINGTON AVE

SAN VICENTE BLVD

FOOD GO

WILSHIRE BLVD

N
W E
S
L.A. SHORTCUTS

Westside/Beaches

183

B.Z.'s Jump

The Eastsider's Westwood Dash from Sunset

(Eastern Approach to Westwood Village)

SHORTCUT TIME:
3 minutes

T. GUIDE PAGES:
32, 41

THE SCOOP

Approaching Westwood Village from any direction is one of the great road challenges left in the 20th Century. Murder and mayhem aptly describe the daily traffic malaise in this area. Complicating the situation is the 400-acre roadblock known as UCLA. Fortunately, on the eastern rim of campus is Hilgard Ave., a no-nonsense mini-freeway that will get you into Westwood quicker than Congress can approve another raise for themselves.

THE ROUTE

Westbound on Sunset Blvd., turn south on Hilgard Ave. Turn west on LeConte Ave. and plow your way into Westwood.

BEST HOURS/DIRECTION

This route cooks 24 hours a day in both directions.

TIPS

Heads up on Hilgard! This is the end-of-the-line for most Santa Monica busses. Their eager-beaver drivers are hard-pressed to park and bail out of these behemoths. We strongly advise you to yield to anything big and blue. (Don't forget that these are company-owned vehicles, and that their drivers just might not care much for you.) Turn down the stereo at Le Conte and Tiverton. This is the UCLA Emergency Medical entrance, so give those ambulances plenty of slack.

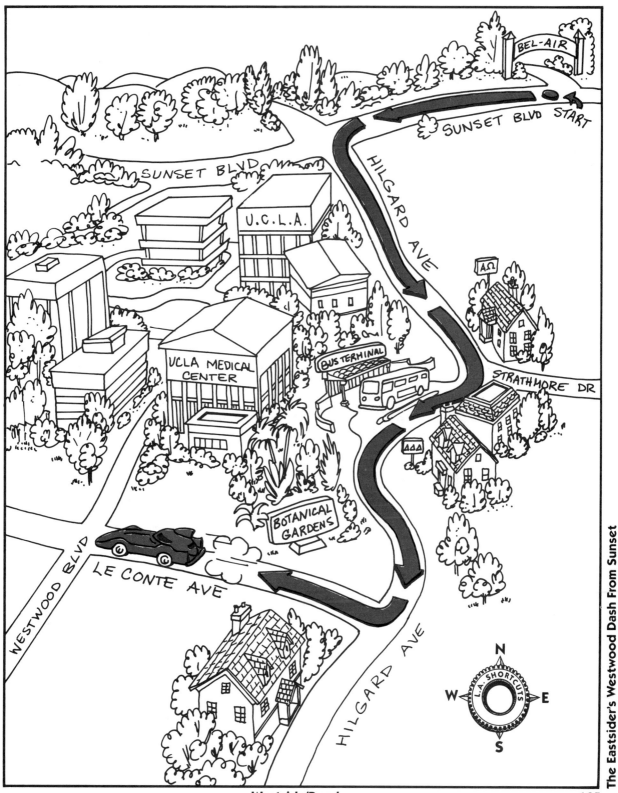

BEL-AIR

SUNSET BLVD START

SUNSET BLVD

HILGARD AVE

U.C.L.A.

UCLA MEDICAL CENTER

BUS TERMINAL

STRATHMORE DR

BOTANICAL GARDENS

WESTWOOD BLVD

LE CONTE AVE

HILGARD AVE

N
W E
S

L.A. SHORTCUTS

The Eastsider's Westwood Dash From Sunset

Freeway Flyer to Westwood

(San Diego Freeway Alternate into Westwood)

<table>
<tr><td><u>SHORTCUT TIME:</u>
3 minutes</td><td align="right"><u>T. GUIDE PAGES:</u>
41, 42</td></tr>
</table>

THE SCOOP

If an award ever celebrated the worst of L.A.'s freeway interchanges, the cloverleaf at the Santa Monica and San Diego Plagueways would take top prize. No matter which direction you're going during rush hour, you're still going nowhere. So how do you make a quick hop into Westwood from the Santa Monica Freeway? Astral projection may work for the metaphysically motivated. For the rest of us, there's Overland Ave.

THE ROUTE

From the Santa Monica Freeway, get off at Overland Ave. Turn north, and turn west on Cushdon Ave., which is two blocks south of Pico Blvd. Turn north onto Westwood Blvd. and jump into the left-hand turn lane. Make a quick left onto Ayres Ave. Turn north onto Veteran Ave and pick up *The Southerner's Approach to Westwood.*

BEST HOURS/DIRECTION

The *Flyer* streaks towards Westwood at all times.

TIPS

Overland turns into its own little freeway between the Santa Monica Freeway and Pico. Stay away from the area around the Westside 'Pudvilion', as teeth-gnashing gear grinders lunge at you from all directions due to the lack of parking.

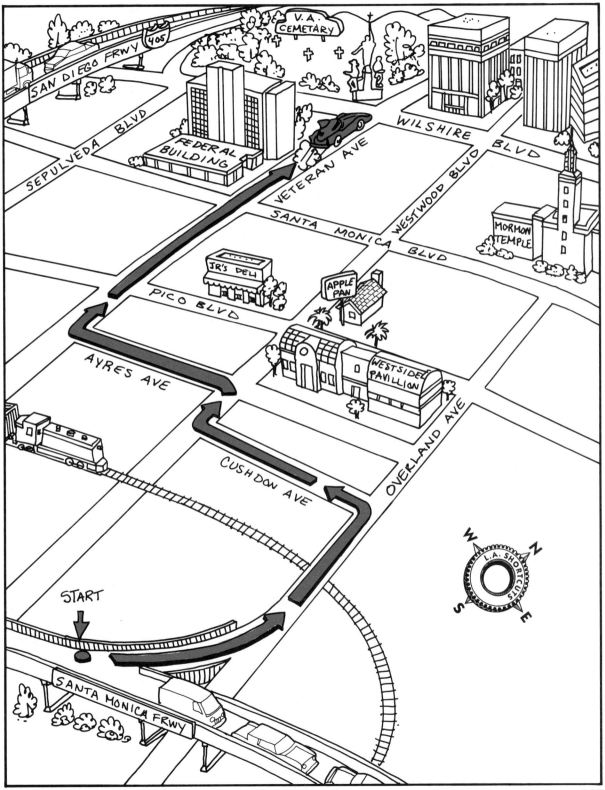

From Rags to Riches
(Venice to Beverly Hills)

SHORTCUT TIME:
17 minutes

T. GUIDE PAGES:
42, 49, 50

THE SCOOP

This route is a microcosm of the American Dream, in that you start at the bottom rung of the socio-economic ladder (Venice) and end up on Easy Street (Beverly Hills). But what normally takes a lifetime to achieve can be experienced vicariously by driving a mere 17 minutes or so. If you motor with The Pack, your path is littered with countless obstacles, such as Wilshire, Olympic, and Pico Blvds. But with our recipe for instant wealth, you can still drive like you're worth a million bucks. When you find it necessary to travel from riches back to rags, we sincerely hope it's accomplished in your car and not in your bank account.

THE ROUTE

Starting at Rose Ave. and Main St. in Venice, follow Rose eastward all the way to Palms Blvd. (Rose turns into Beethoven after the big curve.) Turn east on Palms and continue on after it turns into National Blvd. Turn north on Castle Heights Ave. and follow until you come to Beverwil Dr. Turn north on Beverwil, which turns into Beverly Dr., and in the flip of a billfold, you'll be charging way past your credit limit.

BEST HOURS/DIRECTION

The best time to travel this route is midday. Going east during morning rush hour is a little hectic, but still effective. The same goes for those weary workers heading west in the evening.

TIPS

On Rose, just east of Lincoln, keep an eye out for stray golf balls zooming out of Penmar Golf Course. On clear days bring your camera, because on Palms at Mountainview, there are two great vistas: L.A. to the east, and the Pacific Ocean to the west. Going in either direction, be sure to plow through the Metalheads clogging up the intersections at Sepulveda, Motor, Overland, and Castle Heights.

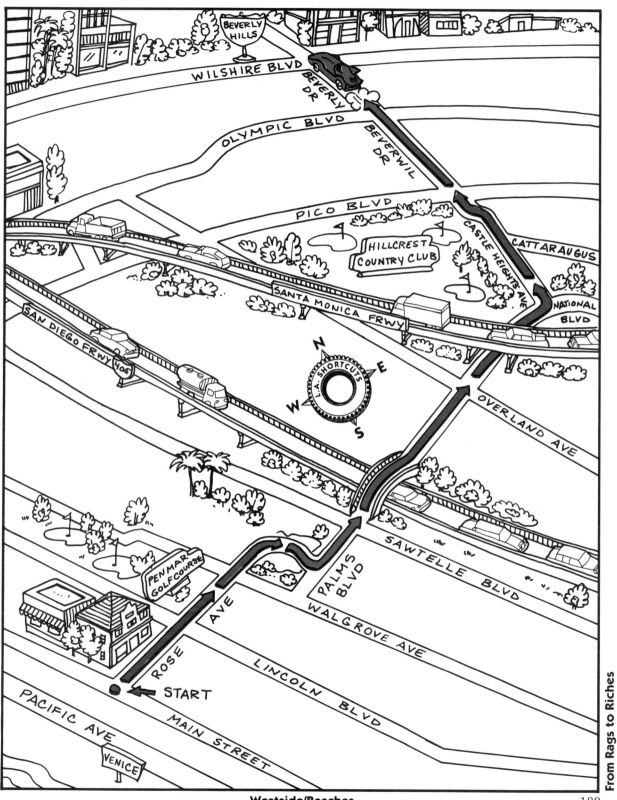

Westside/Beaches

From Rags to Riches

Good-bye Summertime Blues
(Venice/Lincoln Blvds. Beach Crunch Bypass)

THE SCOOP
When Eddie Cochran cranked out his classic hot weather anthem, *"Summertime Blues"*, we think he probably was addressing the daily mobs that deluge Southern California's beaches. Compelled to shoot the tube, millions of beachcombers search highways and low ways for an antidote to this seasonal malaise. Here, for the first time ever in print, is the breakthrough remedy for the beach blockade known as "The Summertime Blues."

THE ROUTE
Eastbound on South Venice Blvd. near the beach, turn right on Washington Way. At the stop sign, turn right on Washington Blvd. (a.k.a. West Washington). At the Kingdom Hall turn left on Woodlawn Ave. and follow until it ends at Grandview Ave. Turn right on Grandview and then make a quick left at Harding Ave. Go one block and turn right onto Naples Ave. Turn left on Coeur D'Alene Ave. and go one block to Lincoln Blvd. Turn south on Lincoln and immediately jump into the left turn lane. Turn east on Zanja St. (at the liquor store) and follow Zanja to Washington Blvd. far ahead of the thong throngs.

BEST HOURS/DIRECTION
One of the few seasonal routes in this book, we recommend this route only during L.A.'s summer months, April through November. Since South Venice is a one-way street, you can use this route only to get out of the beach area.

TIPS
It's going to take some practice to learn this shortcut. There are many quick turns that are easily missed. For the accomplished shortcut artist, the Lincoln Blvd. dogleg presents a worthy challenge — jumping across three lanes of traffic to make a quick left turn.

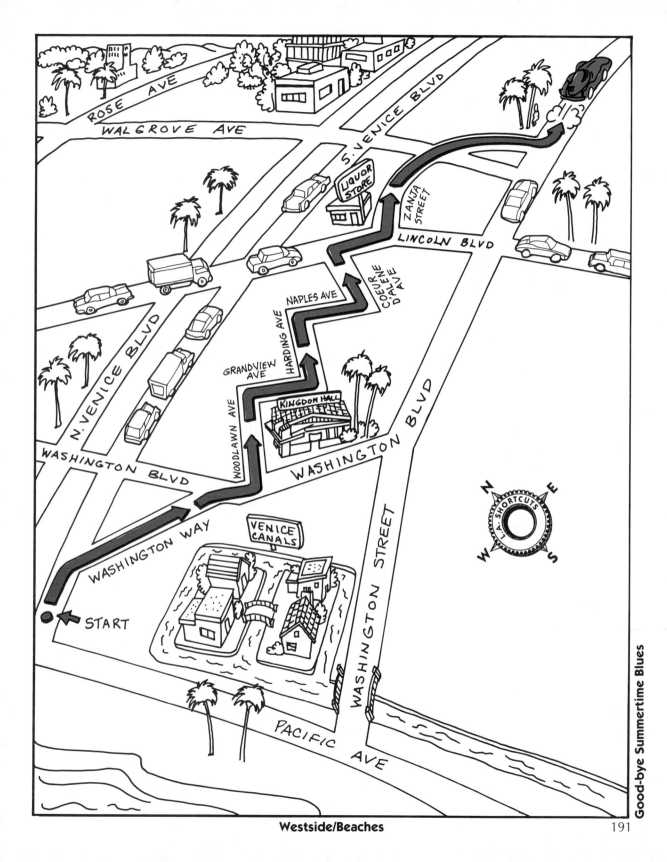

Good-bye Summertime Blues

The Montana Hook Shot
(San Vicente/Wilshire Blvd. Alternate to the Beach)

SHORTCUT TIME:
6 minutes

T. GUIDE PAGES:
40, 41

THE SCOOP
From H.G. Wells to Mr. Peabody and his "Wayback Machine," man and dog have longed to travel backwards in time. Due to the costly hardware involved, few people experience this thrill on a regular basis — until now. We've discovered that a cruise down Montana Ave. will transport you right into an episode of *"Leave It To Beaver."* Montana is a quaint, unspoiled street that imparts a sleepy innocence even upon those who favor quick travel through the area. Resist the urge to drive like you're in the Eisenhower years; you might end up with a flat top and your car could grow tail fins.

THE ROUTE
From San Vicente Blvd. westbound near Bundy, turn west on Montana Ave. Follow Montana all the way to the beach cliffs at Ocean Ave. or any point along the way.

BEST HOURS/DIRECTION
The Hook Shot tends to get a tad congested during evening rush hours, but it's nothing compared to the wolverines on Wilshire Blvd.

TIPS
Just west of Bundy, beware of possible speed traps and the off-angle bank of the road. This curve gets progressively tighter and could cause trouble if you're in a hurry. Budget-conscious shortcutters should stash their checkbook well out of reach; lots of mouth-watering boutiques on Montana reach out and swallow unsuspecting motorists.

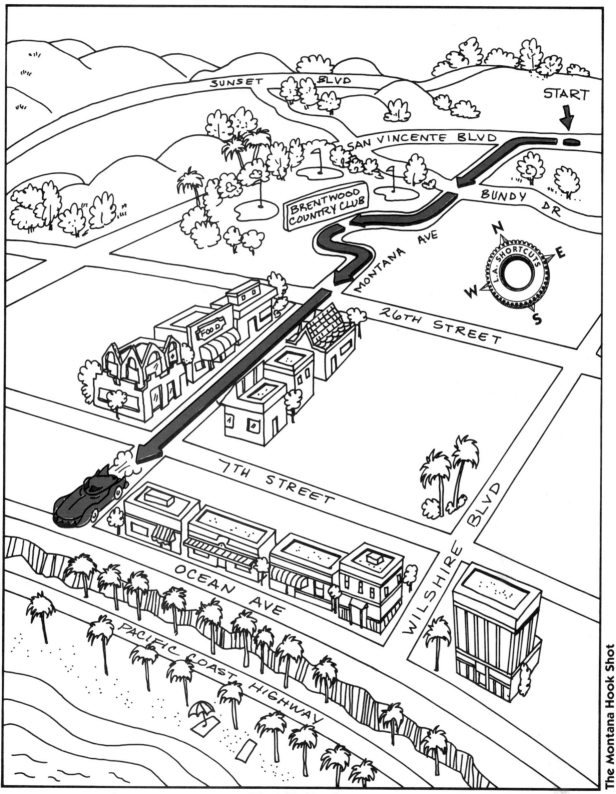

The Montana Hook Shot

Not Pretty, But Fast

(Santa Monica to Venice)

SHORTCUT TIME:
5 minutes

T. GUIDE PAGE:
49

THE SCOOP

Remember the good old days when Main St. was full of derelict missions and biker bars? Beach travel was a breeze. Sadly, the only breeze that remains today is the one that blows in from the Santa Monica Bay — and sometimes even that doesn't smell so good. Rampant development has changed this tiny area into a chic beehive of upscale consumers more concerned with where to shop than how to drive. Lincoln Blvd. and Pacific Ave. are the two likely alternatives to travel through the area. We suggest that you forget 'em both, because right under your nose is a path pioneered by locals —Washington Blvd., also known as West Washington.

THE ROUTE

Westbound from Washington St. in the Marina, turn north on Washington Blvd. Follow it all the way to Main St. Turn right on Main for all points north.

BEST HOURS/DIRECTION

Though more crowded during beach rush hours, this route is great any time of the day in either direction.

TIPS

Take advantage of West Washington while it lasts. It's already doomed to be developed into a carbon copy of Main St. On weekend mornings, watch out for brash broods of pseudo-Italian bicyclists who hog lanes and harass motorists. Suppress your urge to mow them down.

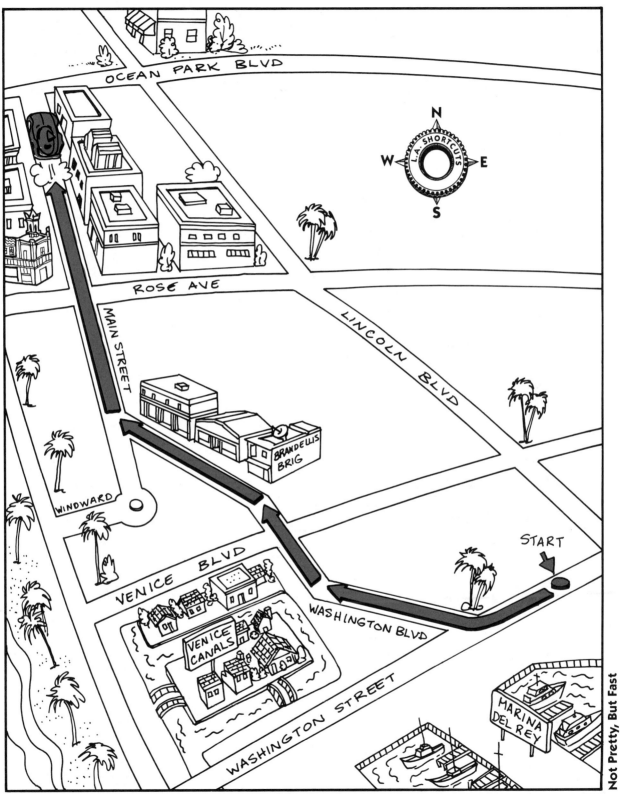

OCEAN PARK BLVD

ROSE AVE

MAIN STREET

LINCOLN BLVD

WINDWARD

BRANDEUIS BRIG

START

VENICE BLVD

WASHINGTON BLVD

VENICE CANALS

WASHINGTON STREET

MARINA DEL REY

N
W E
S

L.A. SHORTCUTS

Not Pretty, But Fast

Oil's Well That Ends Well

(Marina del Rey to Hollywood)

SHORTCUT TIME:
12 minutes

T. GUIDE PAGES:
42, 49, 50

THE SCOOP

Aside from his re-election in 1972, the smoothest endeavor that ex-President Nixon ever was affiliated with was a 1.6 mile stretch of concrete that once bore his name. To Dick's dismay, Caltrans eventually found the moniker an embarrassment, and it was quietly re-christened the Marina Freeway. Following this short-but-sweet concrete ribbon to the east will put you smack in the outer reaches of Baldwin Hills — a mysterious region once thought to be the ends of the earth by early motorists. Even today, superstitious tow truck drivers refuse to aid stranded drivers in the area.

THE ROUTE

Starting in Marina Del Rey, take the Marina Freeway until it ends at Slauson Ave. Turn east on Slauson and continue to Fairfax Ave. and turn north. Turn east on Stocker Ave., then north on La Brea. Take La Brea all the way into Hollywood.

BEST HOURS/DIRECTION

This route is best going north in the morning and south in the evening. Most afternoons, and during the holiday shopping season, you'll hit a traffic clot at Stocker and La Brea. Don't fret; it's still quicker than the 405.

TIPS

Watch your speed on the Marina Freeway; CHP officers love to sneak up on unsuspecting speeders. Don't get caught traveling on Stocker or La Cienega during the next Big Shaker. If you're not fried by the miles of overhead power lines, you'll certainly be blown to bits by the oil and gas deposits in the area. We strongly recommend you to keep a heavy-duty fire extinguisher and thick rubber shoes on hand just in case.

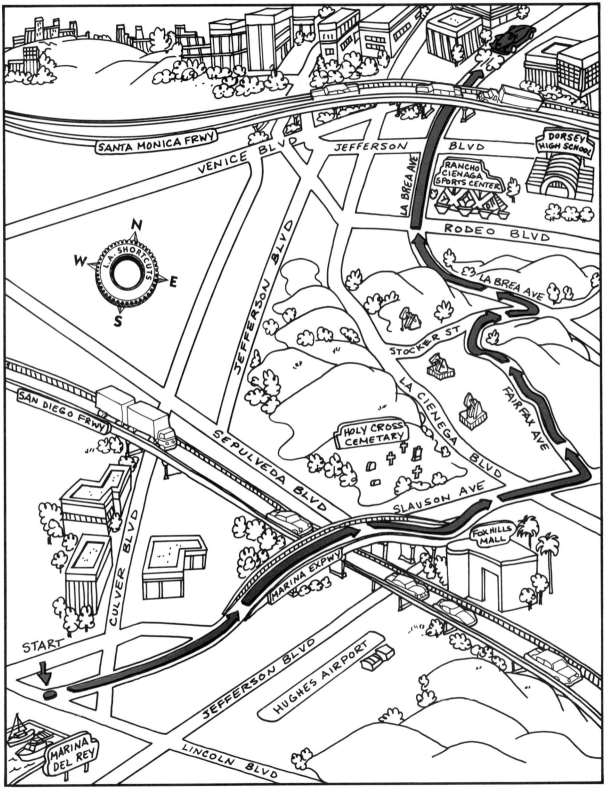

START

MARINA DEL REY

SANTA MONICA FRWY

VENICE BLVD

JEFFERSON   BLVD

LA BREA AVE

DORSEY HIGH SCHOOL

RANCHO CIENAGA SPORTS CENTER

RODEO BLVD

LA BREA AVE

JEFFERSON BLVD

L.A. SHORTCUTS

N
W   E
S

STOCKER ST

FAIRFAX AVE

SAN DIEGO FRWY

SEPULVEDA BLVD

LA CIENEGA BLVD

HOLY CROSS CEMETARY

CULVER BLVD

SLAUSON AVE

FOX HILLS MALL

MARINA EXPWY

JEFFERSON BLVD

HUGHES AIRPORT

LINCOLN BLVD

Oil's Well That Ends Well

The Old Salty Dog's Standby

(East/West Artery from Santa Monica to West L.A.)

SHORTCUT TIME:
8 minutes

T. GUIDE PAGES:
41, 49

THE SCOOP

This is one of the few shortcuts in which the sentimental aspects nearly outweigh the practical applications. Not so long ago, Ocean Park Blvd. was the epitome of the idyllic roadway — a wide-open road that took you to the beach from the Westside. Alas, in a move toward civilizing the north end of Santa Monica Airport, developers installed the shortcutter's arch enemy: traffic signals. They sprung up faster than questions about Vice President Quayle's distinguished National Guard service. Despite all the odds against this fair lane, it still remains one of the quickest ways to get to and from the Westside.

THE ROUTE

Westbound on Pico Blvd. near the 405, turn south onto Gateway Blvd. Gateway turns into Ocean Park Blvd., which goes all the way to the beach.

BEST HOURS/DIRECTION

The *Salty Dog* is best during the morning hours in either direction. Westbound in the evening can get sticky around 23rd St., but hang in there and you'll soon be sipping a cool one at the beach.

TIPS

Early morning and late in the evening between Bundy and 28th St. you're bound to get caught in the stampede of the fitness fanatics. These folks are perpetually late for their workout. Ignore them as they rudely cut in front of you to make a left turn into the Sports Connection. If you're in the mood for some free entertainment, stop near Clover Park, walk over to the far-south end and watch student pilots bounce off the runway.

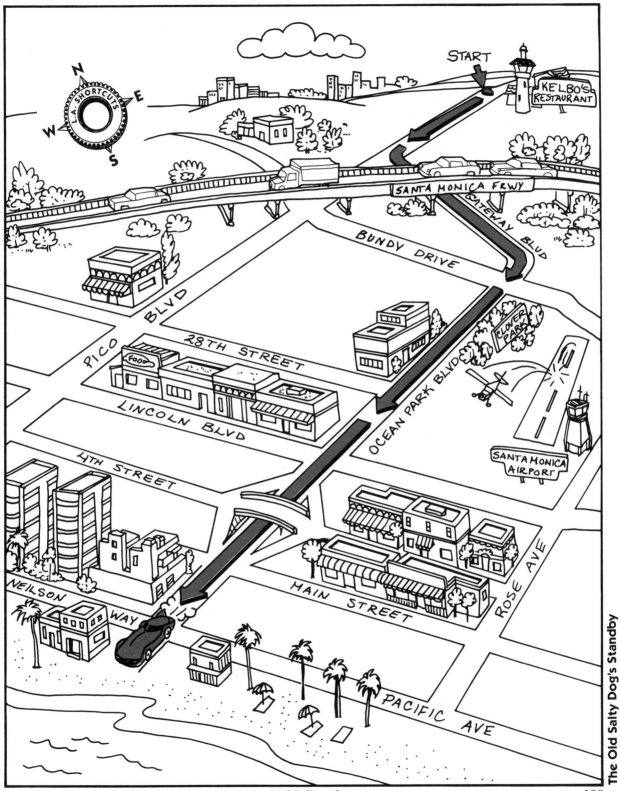

The Old Salty Dog's Standby

One Up the Rear Admiral
(Washington/Lincoln Crowd Detour)

THE SCOOP

If we were to assign a military rank to each of the beach boulevards, none would be worthy of officer's status. While Presidents Washington and Lincoln were exemplary commanders-in-chief, their namesake boulevards trudge with the vitality of a private peeling potatoes on KP duty. To achieve the highest rank in the ocean area's officer's club, we advise you to take *One Up the Rear Admiral*. Admiralty Way will maneuver you around the beachfront battle zone better than Colonel Ollie and company slimed their way around the U.S. Constitution.

THE ROUTE

Eastbound on Washington St., turn south on Via Marina. Get in the left-hand lane and turn east on Admiralty Way. Follow Admiralty all the way to the end, at Fiji Way. Turn east on Fiji, cross Lincoln Blvd., and follow Fiji until it ends at La Villa Marina. Turn left on La Villa Marina and follow it until it ends at Mindinao Way. Turn right on Mindinao and follow it to Alla Rd. Turn north on Alla and follow it to Washington Blvd., where you'll be miles ahead of the gridlock at Washington and Lincoln.

BEST HOURS/DIRECTION

This route wins the Congressional Medal of Honor during prime weekend beach rush hours.

TIPS

You'll have a short wait when making the left turn onto Admiralty from La Via Marina. Once on Admiralty, you'll have to weave through the Lefties and Metalheads at the intersections of Bali and Mindinao. When you get onto Mindinao, you'll hit heavy traffic struggling to get onto the Marina Freeway. Push your way through the throngs and you'll soon be singing *"Anchor's Away."*

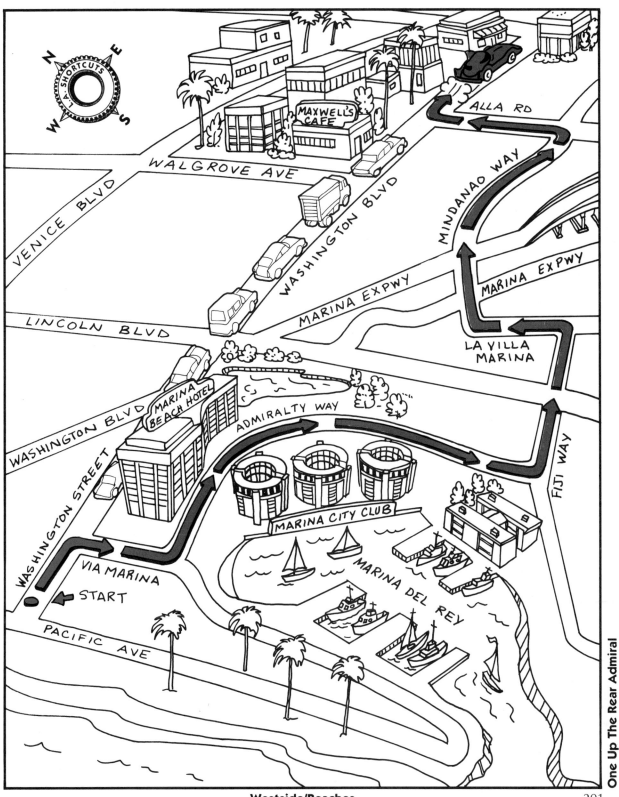

One Up The Rear Admiral

Richard's Back Door Blast to Westwood

(Northern Approach into Westwood)

SHORTCUT TIME:
  4 minutes

T. GUIDE PAGES:
  32, 41

THE SCOOP

There's really only one good thing about going to Westwood: leaving. This quaint "village" is a prime example of city planning run amok, boasting more bottlenecks per square block than anywhere else in the city. Trying to get in and out of Westwood is about as effective as asking Las Vegas for your money back. So what do you do when *"Rocky Meets Godzilla"* screens at 8:00 p.m. and you've got only five minutes to get there? Follow the *Back Door Blast.* We'll get you to the show on time, but if you have to park, plan on attending the 10 o'clock show. It's rumored that petitions are circulating in favor of capping Westwood with a roof, carpeting the streets, and renaming it the Westwood Galleria. Find one and sign it.

THE ROUTE

Eastbound on Sunset Blvd., turn south on Church Lane and follow it to Montana Ave. Turn east on Montana and go four blocks to Levering Ave. Go south on Levering until it turns into Gayley Ave. Notify your next of kin because you now face the bowels of the slogging behemoth known as Westwood.

BEST HOURS/DIRECTION

Considering the options, this route smokes 24 hours a day.

TIPS

Watch out for flying beer cans on Levering as you pass Fraternity Row. Remember, the time saved on this route will be eaten up fighting for a free parking space. We suggest biting the bullet and forking over a few bucks at a parking lot.

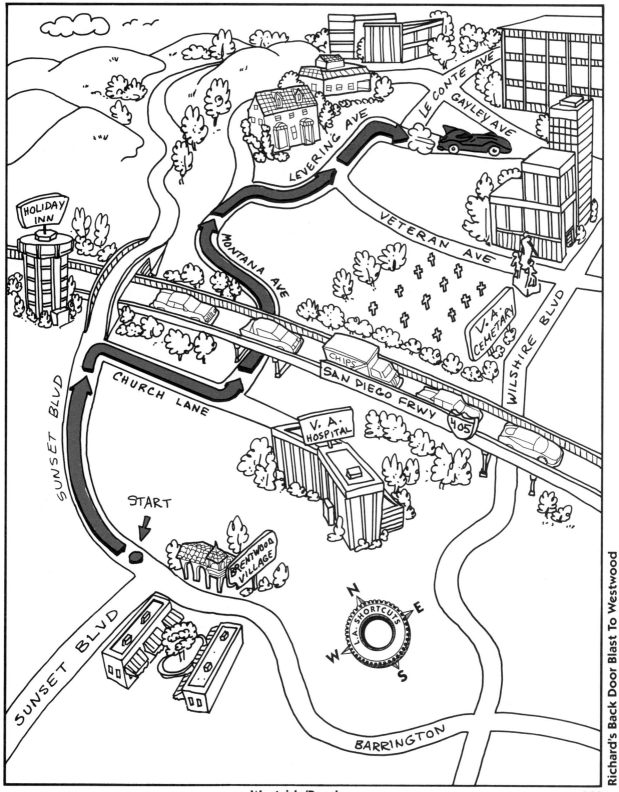

HOLIDAY INN

LEVERING AVE

LE CONTE AVE

GAYLEY AVE

VETERAN AVE

MONTANA AVE

V. A. CEMETERY

WILSHIRE BLVD

SUNSET BLVD

CHURCH LANE

CHIPS

SAN DIEGO FRWY

405

V. A. HOSPITAL

START

BRENTWOOD VILLAGE

SUNSET BLVD

N
E
L.A. SHORTCUTS
W
S

BARRINGTON

The Rustic Run

(Pacific Coast Highway Bypass into Pacific Palisades)

THE SCOOP

If ever there was a shortcut fit for a Sunday drive, this is it! Motoring through Rustic Canyon is a guaranteed antidote for those with traffic migraines. It's also a great reminder for those chasing the almighty dollar that it can be worth the fight. Filled to the brim with exotic foliage and canyon hideaways, this is the place, pocketbook withstanding, where we'd probably all like to live. *The Rustic Run* achieved its short-cut status during the flood-and-fire years of the late 70's. At that time, it was just about the only way into the Palisades when the Pacific Coast Highway was closed.

THE ROUTE

Northbound from Ocean Ave., follow Ocean as it drops down into Santa Monica Canyon. Turn west on West Channel Rd. and go north on Mesa Rd. After the big curve, turn north onto Latimer Rd. Turn west on Brooktree Rd. and continue on to Sunset Blvd.

BEST HOURS/DIRECTION

This placid pathway is great any time of the day.

TIPS

This is not a route to be driven fast. The roads are very narrow and fraught with speed bumps. Unruly drivers have reportedly been pelted by tennis balls and chased out of Rustic Canyon by a bonafide gun-toting posse. If you're trying to get past a roadblock on Sunset during one of the seasonal disasters, refer to the 4th Commandment in our *11 Commandments of the Road*, but don't tell them we told you to.

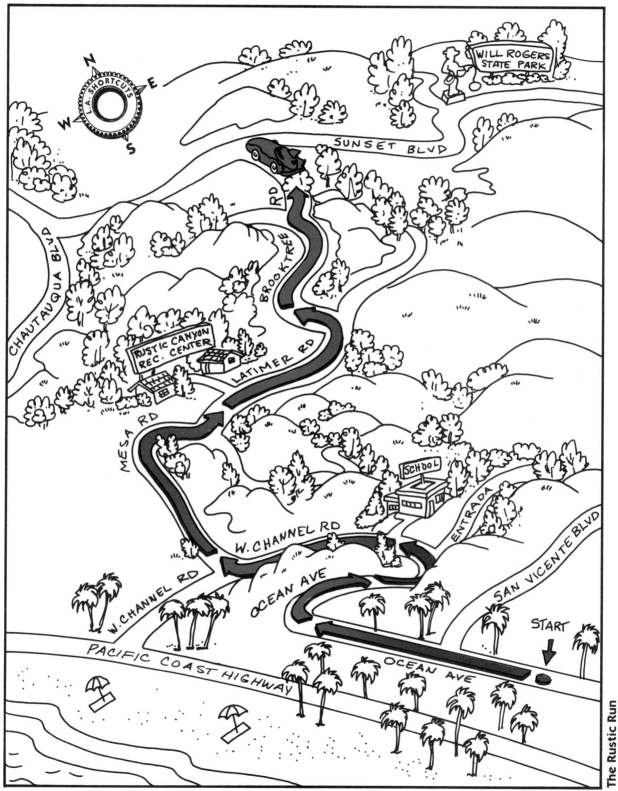

The Rustic Run

Santa Monica's Lost Freeway
(Lincoln Blvd. Alternate Through Santa Monica)

SHORTCUT TIME:
5 minutes

T. GUIDE PAGE:
49

THE SCOOP

There's nothing like a sojourn to the sand to clear out the sinuses and soothe your psyche. Unfortunately, a trip to the beach often lands you in the middle of Lincoln Blvd. wedged between throngs of gum-snapping, towel-toting twits more concerned with how they look than where they're going. Faced with the grim reality of a washed-out surf safari, you're faced with three choices:

1. Next time, leave before the crack of dawn.
2. Save up and build yourself a swimming pool.
3. Jam down 11th St. for all it's worth.

We've found choice #3 to be the least expensive, least exhaustive, and best of all, you'll get to sleep in.

THE ROUTE

Southbound on Lincoln Blvd. in Santa Monica, turn east to 11th St. Turn south on 11th and proceed until to Marine St. Turn west on Marine, cross Lincoln and follow to Highland Ave. Turn right on Highland and then make a quick left back onto Marine. Follow your nose to the beach.

BEST HOURS/DIRECTION

Any time, any day.

TIPS

On 11th Street between Olympic and Ocean Park lurks an occasional SMPD. At Marine and Lincoln you'll encounter a wait at the short-timed traffic light. Hang tough and you'll be at the beach before you know it.

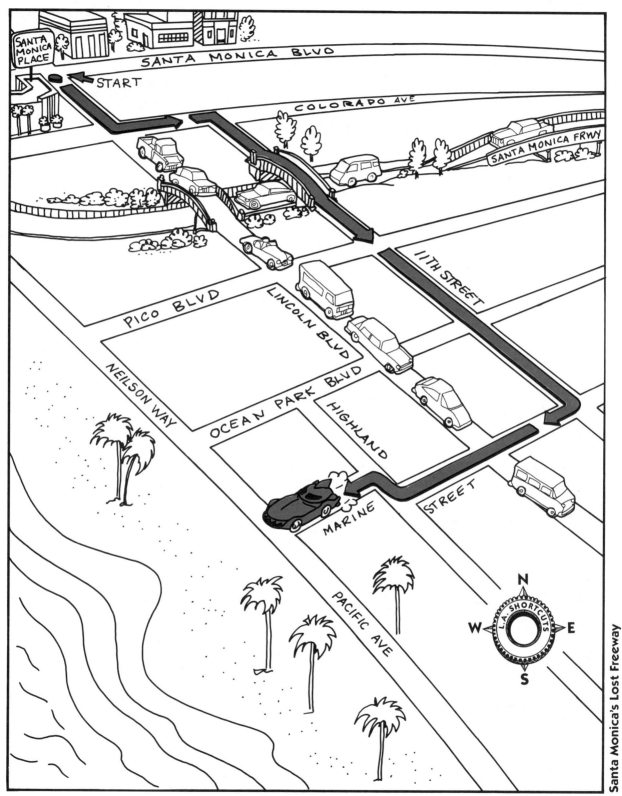

SANTA MONICA PLACE

SANTA MONICA BLVD

START

COLORADO AVE

SANTA MONICA FRWY

PICO BLVD

LINCOLN BLVD

11TH STREET

NEILSON WAY

OCEAN PARK BLVD

HIGHLAND

MARINE

STREET

PACIFIC AVE

N
W E
S

L.A. SHORTCUTS

Santa Monica's Lost Freeway

Westside/Beaches

207

The Southerner's Approach to Westwood

(North/South Westwood Blvd. Bypass into Westwood)

SHORTCUT TIME:
4 minutes

T. GUIDE PAGE:
41

THE SCOOP
When faced with the ugly task of having to get into Westwood on a Friday at 7:30 p.m., most sane people would rather eat a box of nails. Sepulveda is jammed, Wilshire is worse than worthless, and Sunset is nearly always stopped up. Remember our shortcut credo: If you can't blast through the middle, sneak in through the back way. *The Southerner's Approach* may be one of the oldest in the book, but it continues to be one of the all-time back door greats.

THE ROUTE
Traveling east or west on Pico Blvd., turn north on Veteran Ave. until you get to Ohio Ave. Turn east and go one block on Ohio to Kelton Ave. and go north. At the three-way stop intersection, turn left onto Midvale Ave., which turns into Gayley Ave. Proceed into Westwood and the theater line of your choice.

BEST HOURS/DIRECTION
To get the maximum potential from this route, take it only during the worst rush hours, although it still flows smoothly at all other times.

TIPS
Southbound leaving Westwood, be sure to avoid the two right-hand lanes that turn onto Wilshire. (People have been known to celebrate their birthdays twice while waiting in that turn pocket.) When traveling north on Veteran at Santa Monica Blvd. make sure you're in the right-hand lane to avoid the Lefties. At Kelton and Wilshire, don't get stuck in the noon crush of office workers pouring out of the surrounding office towers.

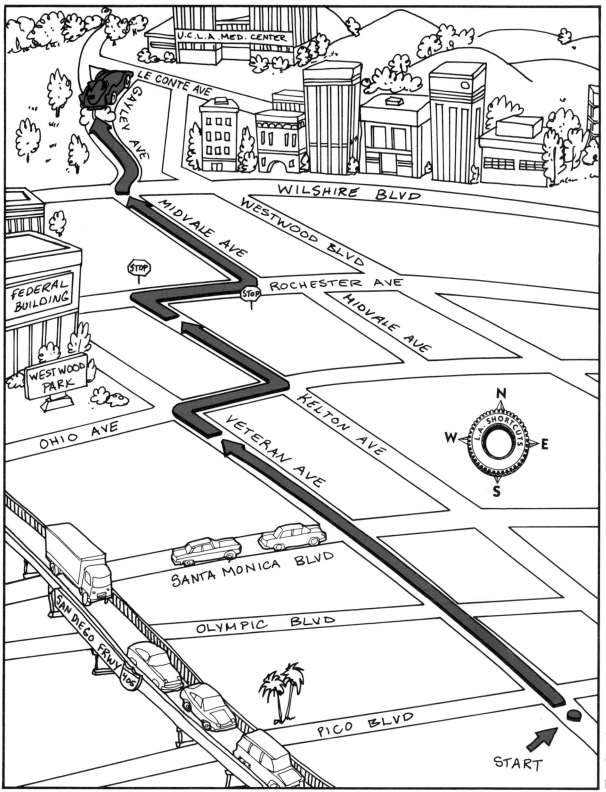

Summa Like It Hot
(San Diego Freeway to Playa del Rey or Marina del Rey)

SHORTCUT TIME:
4 minutes

T. GUIDE PAGES:
49, 50

THE SCOOP

Back in the early 60's, Hughes test pilots had the enviable pleasure of taking in the glorious views of the Ballona Wetlands on their final approach. It was a luxurious greenbelt of meadows and estuaries that stretched from the ocean to the San Diego Freeway. Today, the airfield is gone and the wetlands are doomed to make way for Playa Vista, a gargantuan complex of condos, hotels, and pleasure boat marinas. Score another one for progress. After the dust settles, we hope that the Summa Corp. will have left Jefferson Blvd. untouched. This shortcut streaks along the northern end of the Wetlands faster than a red-tailed hawk diving for a field mouse.

THE ROUTE

Northbound or southbound on the San Diego Freeway, get off at Jefferson Blvd. Head west on Jefferson and mash the pedal to Lincoln Blvd. for all points north, or to continue west to Playa Del Rey.

BEST HOURS/DIRECTION

24 hours a day in either direction.

TIPS

This is a great alternate route for the Marina Freeway on those sweltering summer days. Be sure to stop in at Lopez Ranch for some fresh corn grown right on the premises. The ranch is one of the last holdouts in the area, and could use your support. As the years progress, Jefferson Blvd. looks as if it's becoming the Westwood Blvd. of the Marina area. Use it while it's still tolerable.

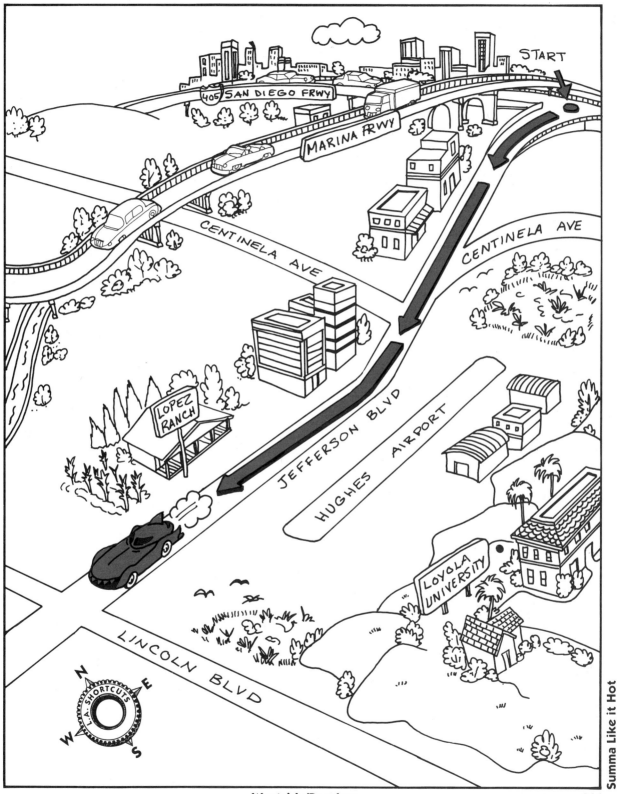

START

405 SAN DIEGO FRWY

MARINA FRWY

CENTINELA AVE

CENTINELA AVE

JEFFERSON BLVD

HUGHES AIRPORT

LOPEZ RANCH

LOYOLA UNIVERSITY

LINCOLN BLVD

L.A. SHORTCUTS

N E W S

Summa Like it Hot

Send Us Your Shortcuts!

Do you have a favorite shortcut you'd like to share with your fellow Shortcut Sharks? Send us your route! If it passes our driving test, we'll name it after you if we include it in the next edition of *L.A. Shortcuts*. Be sure to include the specific directions of the route, hot tips, and any editorial comments you'd care to make. Send your shortcuts to:

L. A. Shortcuts
Box 458
12228 Venice Blvd.
Los Angeles, CA. 90066

Happy Motoring!

Order Form

Do you know someone who drives like a maniac but never arrives where they're going on time? Do you hate the idea of fighting traffic to get them a copy of this book? Join the millions of people who love to shop by mail! Order your extra copies of *L.A. Shortcuts* by using the order form below.

Please send me _____ copies of *L.A. Shortcuts* @ $14.95 each (plus $2.00 postage and handling). I have enclosed a check or money order for $_____ (California residents please add 6.5% sales tax.)

Name: _____

Address: _____

City: _____ State: _____ Zip:_____

Send to:

Red Car Press
Box 458
12228 Venice Blvd.
Los Angeles, CA. 90066

Allow 4-6 weeks for delivery.

This offer subject to withdrawal without notice.